The Cherry Orchard

First published 1978 by Pluto Press Limited
Unit 10 Spencer Court, 7 Chalcot Road, London NW1 8LH

ISBN 0 904383 73 3

Designed by Tom Sullivan

Cover designed by David King

Printed in Great Britain by Latimer Trend & Company Ltd Plymouth

Anton Chekhov

The Cherry Orchard
a new English version
by Trevor Griffiths

from a translation by
Helen Rappaport

Pluto  Plays

The Cherry Orchard

I wrote this new English version of *The Cherry Orchard* in two distinct stages. In the first, I commissioned a new, very literal translation from the Russian, discussed the language and metaphoric life of the play with the translator, tried to map out for myself the specific literary and theatrical problems I would need to solve, and tackled the first act, as a sort of test run. After two months on other work, I entered the second phase, in which I revised parts of the first act before writing the remaining three.

The literary problems were several and oppressive. Chekhov's major status as playwright, his 'poetic sensibility', 'delicate realism' and the rest, seemed for a time major obstacles, inhibiting mediations, in the process of relating freshly and directly to the text itself; and it's impossible to overstress the role played by Helen Rappaport, who made the initial translation, in helping me to distinguish wood from trees in the first phase of the project. But it was the specific nature of Richard Eyre's commission – to prepare a version of the play for *performance* – that proved to be decisive in giving this version its shape, its tone and its texture. For it was not, finally, the *literary* tradition that my version of the play was intended to act upon, but the theatrical. For half a century now, in England as elsewhere, Chekhov has been the almost exclusive property of theatrical class sectaries for whom the plays have been plangent and sorrowing evocations of an 'ordered' past no longer with 'us', its passing greatly to be mourned. For theatregoers, if not for all literary critics (cf. Raymond Williams's penetrating essay in *Drama from Ibsen to Brecht*), Chekhov's tough, bright-eyed complexity was dulced into swallowable sacs of sentimental morality. (The definitive Chekhov movie, in this reading, would have had to be called 'It's a Sad Sad Sad Sad Sad World'.) Translation followed translation, *that* idiom became 'our' idiom, that class 'our' class, until the play's specific historicity and precise sociological imagination had been bleached of all meanings beyond those required to convey the necessary 'natural' sense that the fine will always be undermined by the crude and that the 'human condition' can for all essential purposes be equated with 'the plight of the middle classes'.

I'm speaking here of a dominant mode of translation, performance and production, not of course of all Chekhov work done in this country in this time; but it has been a dominance so oppressive as to distance, especially from the early sixties on, the larger part of a whole generation of theatre writers and workers for whom Chekhov had come to seem, in his content as much as his form, inalienably bound up with the fine regretful weeping of the privileged fallen on hard times. The optimistic among them turned to Brecht, the nihilistic to Beckett, but always at some level as a rejection of Chekhov as a possible comrade in the search for perspectives on the world they live in. And yet who would blame them for failing to see his potency, given the nature of the gelding in the arena.

I can't explain how I never came to see Chekhov in this way. From the age of fifteen, when I had my first exposure to his work via radio, I have always looked *straight through* the productions to the counter-meanings and counter-intentions screaming out to be realised. To come to cases, *The Cherry Orchard* has *always* seemed to me to be dealing not only with the subjective pain of property-loss but also and more importantly with its objective *necessity*. To present it as the first is to celebrate a pessimism; as to see it as both is to redress an important political balance potent in the text Chekhov wrote but in *practice* almost wholly ignored. Readers will judge for themselves whether the version I've written speaks to them more pertinently about the world they live in than other versions they've encountered; but they would have had to *see* it, in a production as truthful as Richard Eyre's at Nottingham, to feel that relevance bite into the flesh, since plays, unlike theses, require more of us than careful reflection and analysis: they demand to be *experienced*, on both sides of the text, with actors and audience both listening and making, which is arguably now the only truly *social* validity theatre can lay claim to in a television age.

Those familiar with the play in other versions (and productions) have claimed, though on the whole with considerable sympathy, that my version has shifted the focus of the play and re-ordered its inherent balances; so that, for example, Mme Ranevsky's pivotal role has been reduced, while Trofimov's – and to some extent Lopakhin's – have been strengthened. There isn't space here to argue this fully, but the simple *facts* are that (a) I *edited out* next to nothing, save for some patronymics (though I debated hard about the often unplayably expository structure of Act One); (b) I *added* fewer than fifty words of dialogue to a play that has approximately 21,000; (c) not a single line or action was transposed to another part of the play. If Ranevsky seems less 'important' in my version, and Trofimov and Lopakhin (and the ideo-logical tension between them) more central to an understanding of the play's meanings, let it be Chekhov who answers for it, not me.

Less gentle critics, I should add, have hinted that I found what I was look-ing for rather than what was there; that I substituted, for an elegy, a cheerful and cheering march. My answer might well be 'Don't make me laugh' save for the possibility that, given *their* view of Chekhov, I might well be accused of stealing their line. For to dare to see his world as both subjectively painful and objectively comic is somehow, for them, to fail to sound the right note or to play 'The Last Post' as punk rock. It's to these last, 'high priests of the sacred art' as Trepleff calls them in *The Seagull*, that I'd like to dedicate this new version of their favourite play, in the hope that by reading it they'll come to question one of the central tenets of their faith; namely, that Anton Chek-hov, that lively class heretic, can continue to be considered one of the faithful.

Trevor Griffiths,
Boston Spa, September 1977

This version of Anton Chekhov's **The Cherry Orchard** was
first performed at the Nottingham Playhouse on 10 March 1977,
with the following cast:

Mme Ranevsky (Liuba): landowner	Bridget Turner
Gayev (Leon)	Ralph Nossek
Simeonov-Pischik (Boris)	Brian Glover
Lopakhin (Alexander)	Dave Hill
Anya	Lynsey Baxter
Varya	Annie Hayes
Charlotte	Susan Porrett
Epikhovdov (Simon)	Antony Sher
Dunyasha	Helen Brammer
Firs (Nicholas)	John Barrett
Yasha	Malcom Storry
Other servants	Frank Robinson
	Walter Lindley
	Julian Webber
Trofimov (Peter)	Mick Ford
Stationmaster	John C. Williams
Guests	Jo Scott-Matthews
	Peggy Pedley
	Walter Lindley
	Eric Parker
Stranger	David Beames
Charlotte's dog	Craiglyn Cavalcade

Stage Manager: Frank Robinson
Deputy Stage Manager: Heather Lillicrap
Directed by Richard Eyre
Set designed by John Gunter
Costumes designed by Pippy Bradshaw
Lighting by Rory Dempster

ACT I

Black.

A slow gathering of light reveals a single cherry tree in flower. The image steadies; holds. A long way away, the sound of a steel cable groaning under stress.

Closer, though still distant, a train whistles its approach.

Silence.

Fade to black.

Black.

Tape: (LOPAKHIN's *voice*): «Пришёл пóезд, слáва Бóгу. Котóрый час?»

Early dawn light reveals the old nursery, several doors leading from it, one to ANYA's *room. May. Frost. Shut windows.* LOPAKHIN, *late thirties, strong-shouldered, bearded, in suit, white shirt, light calf-skin boots, sprawls uneasily in a winged chair, an open book across his chest, sleeping fitfully. The sound of the train's whistle wakes him.* DUNYASHA *comes in, carrying a lit candle, as* LOPAKHIN *fumbles for his watch.*

Lopakhin That's the train. At last. What's the time?

Dunyasha Two nearly. (*Blows out candle.*) It's day.

Lopakhin (*Checking watch.*) Only two hours behind time, this one. Mmm. (*Stands, yawns, stretches.*) God, look at me. Come here on purpose to meet them all at the station and ptt . . . wake up to find I've been asleep . . . This won't do at all, Lopakhin.

He watches DUNYASHA, *who's rather pointlessly dusting the furniture, her mind elsewhere.*

Why didn't you waken me?

Dunyasha (*Listening for something.*) I thought you'd gone . . . Oh, it's them, they're coming.

Lopakhin (*Listening briefly, tries to straighten trouser creases.*) No, no . . . They have to get the luggage, find the tickets, be greeted by the station-master . . .

He sits down again, to polish his boots with a handkerchief, his back to DUNYASHA, *who has crossed, excited, to the window.*

Five years she's been away, I wonder what she looks like. (*Chuckles*) She's a good woman, easy-going, no side.

The dogs begin to bark in the yard, DUNYASHA *leaves unnoticed to tend them.*

I remember when I was a lad, fifteen mebbe, my father ran that little grocer's in the village, he punched me in the face with his fist – (*shows his fist*) – and my nose were bleeding, we'd come up to this place for something, I can't remember what, *he* was drunk, I remember that . . . (*Stops polishing shoes, stares ahead of him.*) . . . and *she* said, thin little, young little thing that she was, she said, 'No need for tears, little peasant. It'll heal before your wedding day.' And she washed the blood from my face, here, in the nursery.

He stands, inspects his boots and trousers.

And here I am, a rich man, in white waistcoat and yellow boots, but the son of a peasant still, with my pig's snout in the teacup . . .

DUNYASHA *comes back in, with a shawl on, again unnoticed, returns to window.* LOPAKHIN *laughs, turns.*

This book put me to sleep, couldn't understand a word.
Dunyasha Those dogs have howled all night. They know who's coming home . . .

LOPAKHIN *sniffs, not understanding, frowns.*

Lopakhin Dogs? What's wrong with you, Dunyasha. You're all . . .
Dunyasha Look at my hands. I think I'm going to faint.
Lopakhin (*Gently*) Here, come here. (*Takes her hands gently; amused.*) Look at you. (*Fingers her shawl.*) You dress like a lady, do your hair like one too. You're much too refined, Dunyasha. We have to remember what we are, mm?

She blinks at him, calmer. EPIKHODOV *comes in, boots squeaking, looking for someone, a bunch of flowers in his hands. Sees* DUNYASHA, *half-presents them to her, sees* LOPAKHIN, *drops them. Picks them up.*

Epikhodov The gardener sent them. He says they're for the dining-room. Here.

He hands them to DUNYASHA, *tender-brusque.*

Lopakhin I'll have some cider while you're about it.
Dunyasha Very good, sir.

She leaves.

Epikhodov (*Pacing a little, squeaking.*) It's a morning, er . . . it's a *frosty* morning. Three degrees. Er, below. (*Waving awkwardly at the window.*) And yet the cherry trees are all . . . in bloom. I do not approbate this climate of ours. I do not. Unco-operative and untimely, that's what it is. Another thing, Alexander Lopakhin, by way of footnote – (*he stares at his feet*) – let me tell you I bought these boots the day before yesterday but they travel – I assure you – beyond the bounds of possibility. (*They* *squeak very slightly, as he shifts weight.*) Would grease help, do you think? . . .

Lopakhin Go away. You bore me.

Epikhodov Every day of my life I befall something dreadful. But no longer do I grumble. Now I even smile sometimes . . .

DUNYASHA *has entered, handed* LOPAKHIN *the cider. His eyes follow her.*

Well, I'll be off . . . (*Falls disastrously over a chair.*) Aah, see. If you'll excuse my language, that's . . . (*Long pause.*) . . . the sort of thing . . . I had in mind . . . Beware the clam before the storm. At least in my opinion.

He squeaks off.

Dunyasha If you promise you'll keep a secret, Mr Lopakhin . . .

LOPAKHIN *nods.*

. . . Epikhodov has asked me to marry him.

Lopakhin Ah.

This slides effortlessly into a yawn; DUNYASHA *misses it.*

Dunyasha I really can't make up my mind what to do. He's quiet really, but when he gets started, I mean you can't make head or tail of it. I mean it's very nice and . . . I mean and even . . . moving . . . except I can't understand a word he says. I mean I quite like him. And he loves me to distraction, of course. Such a sad man. Every day something else befalls him. So everyone teases him and calls him . . . (*Laughing*) . . . 'Million Miseries' . . .

Lopakhin Sh. That's them. (*Listens. We hear nothing. He nods.*) Ahunh.

Dunyasha (*Galvanised and paralysed.*) They're here! They're here! What do I do? Look at my hands.

Lopakhin Yes, they've arrived. Let's go and meet them at the door. I wonder if she'll even know me, after five years . . .

Dunyasha I'll faint, this minute, I know I will.

She follows LOPAKHIN *from the room. Sounds of carriages drawing up before the house. Doors. Sounds of people in farther rooms.* FIRS *crosses the room in the other direction at slow speed, leaning on a stick. He wears old-style livery and a top hat. He mutters to himself throughout, but unintelligibly. Voices getting nearer. One calls,* 'No, we can go through here!' MME RANEVSKY *comes in, followed by* ANYA, CHARLOTTE, *with a dog on a lead, all dressed in travelling clothes,* VARYA, *in coat and headscarf,* GAYEV, PISCHIK, LOPAKHIN, DUNYASHA *with small bag and umbrella, and* SERVANTS *carrying luggage.* ANYA *pushes ahead to take the centre of the room.*

Anya You remember *this* room, Mother.

Mme Ranevsky (*As though racking her brains.*) The er . . . (*Changes suddenly, smiling.*) . . . nursery.

Varya It's rather cold, I'm afraid. (*Rubbing the backs of her thin white hands.*) Your rooms – the white one and the blue one – are exactly as you left them, Mother.

Mme Ranevsky (*Deep in the room now, her arm on* ANYA's *shoulder.*) Look. The nursery. My dear and lovely room. I was a child here. And I'm a child again . . . (*She kisses* GAYEV.) Remember, brother? Mmm. And you haven't changed at all, Varya – (*kisses her*) – my little nun. (*Over* VARYA's *shoulder.*) Dunyasha?

DUNYASHA *nods, curtseys, excited to be recognised.*

Gayev Two hours late, that train. What a way to run things!

Charlotte (*To* PISCHIK, *who's stroking the dog's ears.*) It eats nuts.

Pischik (*Withdrawing slightly.*) Imagine.

They all leave, except for ANYA *and* DUNYASHA. DUNYASHA *begins to remove* ANYA's *coat and hat.*

Dunyasha It's been a long wait . . .

Anya I haven't slept for four nights . . . It's so *cold.*

Dunyasha (*Rubbing* ANYA's *hands.*) You left in winter, you come back in spring . . . and it's not changed at all. My lovely . . . (*Kisses her shyly.*) We're done with waiting, my lovely. Now, I've something to tell you that can't wait . . .

Anya (*Tired, barely listening.*) I'm sure you have.

Dunyasha I've had a proposal.

Anya Really.

Dunyasha From Epikhodov. The clerk.

Anya (*Sitting down, exhausted.*) Dunyasha, Dunyasha. (*Fiddling with her hair.*) There's not a pin left.

Dunyasha I wish I knew what to do. He really is mad about me.

Anya (*Staring through door at her room.*) My room, windows . . . Have I been away at all? Home. And the orchard . . . the first place I'll go, tomorrow. But first I must sleep. I didn't sleep the whole journey. I've been so anxious . . .

Dunyasha Mr Trofimov arrived two days ago.

Anya Peter!

Dunyasha He's putting up in the wash-house. He says he doesn't want to put on anybody. (*Looking at watch.*) I know he'd want me to wake him, but Miss Varya said I mustn't. (VARYA's *tones.*) 'Don't you wake him,' she said.

VARYA *comes in, a bunch of keys at her waist.*

Varya Dunyasha, coffee. Quickly, girl . . . Mama is asking for coffee.

Dunyasha I'm going, I'm going. (*Leaves*)

Varya Well, thank God you're home. You're back home again.

Strokes ANYA's *temples, rhythming the endearments.*

My most dear, most pure, most precious sister's back again.

Anya It's been . . . (awful).

Varya (*Soothing* ANYA's *forehead, eyelids.*) I know, I know.

Anya Passion Sunday I left. I thought I'd die of cold on the train. And Charlotte either gabbled or did card tricks all the way to Paris. I told you not to saddle me with her.

Varya You're seventeen, child. You couldn't have travelled alone.

Anya We arrive in Paris. It's snowing. My French is useless. Mother's living in a fifth-floor apartment and when I arrive she has some French people visiting her, some ladies, an old priest with a Bible in his hand, the room's dingy and full of cigarette smoke. (*Pause*) I just suddenly – I felt so sorry for her – I just suddenly took Mama's head in my hands and held on tight and couldn't let go. And Mama . . . hugged me. Cried.

Varya Sh. That's enough.

Anya She'd sold the villa in the south before I arrived and she was still penniless. And I only just made it to Paris, so I wasn't much help. But it made no difference. We had dinner in the most expensive restaurants and she'd order the most expensive dishes and make the waiters rich men overnight with her tips. Charlotte was just as bad. It was appalling. (*Afterthought*) *And* Yasha. He's mother's valet now, you know; so he had to come back with us.

Varya (*Frosty*) Yes, I noticed him.

Anya (*Straightening.*) Well then. What about here? Have we paid the interest?

Varya With what?

Anya None of it?

Varya They're putting the estate up for auction in August.

Anya Dear Jesus!

LOPAKHIN *puts his head round the door, clucks like a chicken, leaves.*

Varya (*Startled, angered.*) Holy Mother of God, I could . . .

She clenches her fists, staring at the doorway.

ANYA *takes her fists, strokes them into hands again.*

Anya What about Lopakhin? Has he asked you yet?

VARYA *shakes her head once, curt.*

Why don't you have it out with him. Isn't he supposed to love you?

Varya There's nothing there. He's too busy with his . . . business. He has no time for me. Barely notices I'm in the room. I can't take any more . . . There's great talk about the impending wedding, him and me, I'm congratulated all the time, but in reality . . . there's nothing, it's just . . . a dream. (*She fingers a brooch on* ANYA'*s bosom.*) Where did you get that? What is it, a bee?

Anya Mama bought it. For the journey home. It cost a fortune!

She laughs suddenly, goes into her room. Her voice is gay now, almost carefree.

Guess what? In Paris, I went up in a balloon!

Varya (*Following as far as the door.*) And now you are home, precious one.

DUNYASHA *comes in with a coffee pot. Begins to make coffee.*

Dunyasha (*Importantly.*) Coffee.

Varya (*At* ANYA'*s door, looking in.*) You know what I do as I go about my jobs around the house? I dream. I dream you were going to marry a rich man. I dream that I could then retreat from all this, to some remote convent somewhere, and leave it only to make pilgrimages to holy places, Kiev, Moscow, on and on. Such peace it would bring . . .

Anya (*Listening.*) The birds. Listen. In the garden. What time is it?

Varya Past two. Time you were in bed, dear child. (*Going into* ANYA'*s room.*) It would bring such peace.

YASHA *comes in, with travelling rug and case. He stands for a moment, self-importantly surveying the scene.* DUNYASHA *is filtering the coffee.*

Yasha (*Affectedly refined air.*) Excuse me, Madame, is one permitted to pass this way . . .?

Dunyasha (*Staring at him.*) My, haven't you changed though, Yasha. I barely recognised you.

Yasha I'm sorry, I don't think I've had the . . .

Dunyasha Dunyasha! When you went away I was this high. (*Shows him with her hand.*) Fydor Kozeyodov's daughter. Don't you remember?

Yasha (*Closing in, inspecting her.*) Hmmm. (*Sniffs*) Quite a . . . cucumber!

YASHA *checks the doors with a glance. Puts his hands under her arms and cups her breasts. She yelps, drops a saucer.* YASHA *evaporates.*

Varya (*In the doorway, cross.*) What's going on?

Dunyasha (*Upset*) I dropped a saucer.

Varya (*Crosses herself.*) Let's hope it bodes well. (*Pause.* DUNYASHA *crosses herself.*) Pick it up then.

Anya (*Re-entering*) We should warn Mama Peter Trofimov's here.

Varya He won't be wakened, it's all right. I've given orders.

Anya But *she* must know, Varya. Think what might happen if he were to walk in on her unannounced. Father dying. Grisha drowning in the river. Mother abandoning us, fleeing to Paris, all that grief, all that guilt flooding back . . . Even now, six years later, she still won't believe she's forgiven . . . whatever one tells her . . .

FIRS *comes in. He wears a jacket over a white waistcoat. Advances laboriously on the coffee pot.*

Firs The mistress will take her coffee here. (*Puts on white gloves*) Is it ready? (*Looks around the table. To* DUNYASHA, *sharp.*) Hey! Cream!
Dunyasha Oh my God!

She hurries off excitedly.

Firs (*Fussing*) Witless wench! (*Muttering to himself.*) They've arrived...a hunh ... all the way from Paris . . . the master used to go to Paris . . . I remember that . . . ahunh, yes he did . . . In a coach (*Laughs suddenly.*)
Varya Who are you talking to, Firs?
Firs (*Mishearing*) Almost three, Ma'am. (*Happy*) The mistress is home, the long wait is over, now I can die. (*Begins to weep with happiness.*)

Enter MME RANEVSKY, GAYEV, PISCHIK. PISCHIK *wears a long Russian coat of fine cloth, wide trousers tucked into his boots.* GAYEV *mimes billiard shots, very seriously.*

Mme Ranevsky (*Laughing a little.*) Let's see if I can remember how it goes now. Pot into the corner pocket, double off the cush – –
Gayev *Cut*, sister, cut into the corner! (*Taken suddenly by the room.*) Ah . . . We used to sleep in here as children, if I'm not . . . And now, odd as it may seem, I'm fifty-one.
Lopakhin (*Ironic*) Yes. Tempus fugit.
Gayev What?
Lopakhin Time . . . (*lamely*) . . . flies.
Gayev (*Glaring*) Stinks of patchouli in here.
Anya I'm for bed. (*Kissing* MME RANEVSKY.) Good night Maman.
Mme Ranevsky (*Kissing her hands.*) Mmm. Sweet child. Aren't you glad to be home. I'm still a little dazed by it all.
Anya Uncle.
Gayev (*Kissing her cheek and hand.*) Bless you just like your mother. You were just like her at her age, Liuba.

ANYA *shakes hands with* LOPAKHIN *and* PISCHIK *and leaves, shutting her door behind her.*

Mme Ranevsky She's worn out.
Pischik The journey.

Pause. Silence. A sort of blankness settles. FIRS *mutters something nobody hears. Silence again.*

Varya Well then, gentlemen. It's late. Time you were gone.
Mme Ranevsky (*Laughing suddenly.*) Varya, you haven't changed a bit.

Draws her to her, kisses her brow.

I'll just drink my coffee and then we'll all go.

FIRS *places a cushion under her feet.*

Thank you, my dear.

She waits while FIRS *regains his feet, a tightrope performance but in the subtlest miniature.*

I've grown used to it, you know. (*Shows cup.*) Coffee. Drink it all the time. (*To* FIRS, *swaying still, but upright.*) Thank you, dear old man. (*She kisses him on the brow.*)

Varya I ought to check the luggage is all there. (*Leaves*)

Mme Ranevsky Is this really me, sitting here like this? (*Excited*) Oh, I feel like . . . dancing, I feel like dancing! If it's a dream, don't waken me. Because . . . I love this place. I love it so much I couldn't see it properly from the train. For tears. (*Pause*) Coffee. (*She drains the cup.*) Thank you, Firs, thank you, dear old man. It's good you still live.

Firs Not yesterday. Day before.

Gayev But deaf.

FIRS *mumbles his way to the coffee table.*

Lopakhin (*Checking watch.*) I have to catch a train to Kharkov in an hour. Pity. I wanted a good look at you. And a talk. (*Pause*) You're as magnificent as ever.

Pischik And even more beautiful! *A la mode*, is it? I swear my heart's not stopped pounding like a race horse's since she arrived.

Lopakhin (*Slight awkwardness.*) Your brother here, Leon, says I'm a boor, a kulak, but it doesn't hurt me. He's welcome to his opinion. All I ask is that *you* trust me as before, hold me in the same regard as before. My father was serf to yours and to his father, too. But you've done so much for me, you've helped me forget all that . . . history . . . and love you . . . as my own sister More, perhaps.

MME RANVESKY *stands, cup in hands, crosses to the table, where* FIRS *laboriously pours another cup of coffee.*

Mme Ranevsky I can't sit still, forgive me. (*Paces room a little, touching things. Laughs suddenly.*)

This happiness is insufferable. Laugh if you like, I know it's silly. (*She presses the bookcase with her cheek.*)

My own bookcase. (*Strokes table.*)

(My own table. (*Kisses it.*)

Gayev Nurse died while you were away.

Mme Ranevsky Yes, I know. May she rest in God's arms. They wrote me.

Crosses to her seat, coffee in hands.

Gayev Anastasi died too. Oh, and Peter . . . erm . . . the one with the squint
. . . handed in his notice. He's joined the police force.

Takes a box of sweets from his pocket, removes one, sucks it.

Pischik My daughter . . . Dashenka . . . sends her . . . regards.

Lopakhin Mme Ranevsky is right, this is no time for gloom. Let me cheer you
up with this. (*Checking watch.*) There isn't time for a full discussion – I
can't miss my train – but here it is in essence. The cherry orchard is down
to be sold by auction to pay off your debts. This much you know. Now,
the date of the auction has been set for August the twenty-second. (MME
RANEVSKY *puts down her cup suddenly.*)

But you can go to your bed tonight and dream pleasant dreams, because
there's a way out. Now listen. Your land is less than twenty miles from
town *and* near the railway, right? If the orchard and the land by the river
were to be parcelled up into plots and leased out for weekend cottages,
you'd have a per annum yield of twenty-five or even thirty thousand.
What about that!

Gayev Bloody nonsense. Absolute bloody . . . (*He internalises his thought
suddenly.*)

Mme Ranevsky I'm not sure I understand . . . what you're saying, Mr . . .

Lopakhin How do I get the yield figure? Well, look, you can ask at least ten
roubles per year per acre plot, and if you put it on the market right away
there won't be a plot left by the autumn, take the word of a man who
knows. In fact, dear lady, you are to be congratulated: you're com-
prehensively saved. It's a fine location; bathing to be had in the river.
All you'll have to do is a bit of . . . cleaning and tidying. All those out-
buildings and things will have to go, of course . . . and this place too,
which is of only marginal value to anyone now. And the cherry orchard.

Mme Ranevsky The cherry orchard what?

Lopakhin Five men could clear it in . . . (*calculates*) . . . less than a week . . .

Mme Ranevsky Cut it down? How . . . Forgive me, you appear not to understand . . . If there is one truly remarkable thing in this entire region it is
my cherry orchard.

Lopakhin Forgive me, Mme Ranevsky, but the only remarkable thing about
your cherry orchard is its dimensions. It's very large. But there is nothing
at all remarkable in producing a crop every other year which nobody
actually wants.

Gayev This orchard has an entry to itself in the *Encyclopaedia Russkaya*.

Lopakhin (*Deliberately, looking at his watch.*) All right. But unless there's
some pretty clear thinking and some sensible decisions forthcoming,
both it and the estate will come under the hammer on the twenty-second

of August. (*Pause. Carefully.*) You will have to make up your minds. (*Pause*) But be assured: there is no other way out. None at all.

He's ready to go, but not able. GAYEV *is agitated, pacing a little,* PISCHIK *is half-asleep,* MME RANEVSKY *pale, ghostly. A bird sings, rather brightly, in the lightening orchard beyond the windows.*

Firs Once upon a time they would dry the cherries, preserve them in jars, or turn them into jam, or sometimes even . . .

Gayev Shut up, please, Firs.

Firs . . . and sometimes even send them dried, you see, in carts, to Moscow and Kharkov. People wanted them then. I can still smell them sometimes, soft and sweet, the dried cherries. They knew how to do it then . . .

Mme Ranevsky (*Softly*) And now?

Firs Forgotten now. No one remembers.

Pischik How was the food in Paris then, eh? Did you eat frogs?

Mme Ranevsky I ate crocodiles.

Pischik (*Uncertainly*) Imagine.

Lopakhin The recipe for drying cherries is no longer the point, Mme Ranevsky. Once there were just masters and serfs in these parts: now there are weekenders, holidaymakers. And twenty years from now there'll be masses of them, in summer cottages, round every town, even the smallest. As of now they just . . . drink tea on their verandahs, but I see a day when these same people will take to planting out their little acre, growing things, and the orchards will . . . live again, will be alive again with growing things . . .

Gayev Bloody nonsense. Absolute bloody . . .

VARYA *comes in,* YASHA *behind her.*

Varya (*Crossing to bookcase, selecting key as she walks.*) I forgot the telegrams that came for you, Mama. (*Finding them.*) Here they are.

GAYEV *has followed* VARYA *to the bookcase, placed his hands on its sides.* MME RANEVSKY *studies the telegrams briefly, then tears them up.*

Mme Ranevsky Paris. I've forgotten Paris.

Gayev Do you know how old this bookcase is, Liuba? The other day I was rummaging in this bottom drawer and noticed some figures burned in the wood. Eighteen hundred and three. A hundred years ago, mmm? Perhaps we should celebrate its centenary. True it's . . . inanimate, a . . . thing, yet it remains, a bookcase.

Pischik (*Impressed*) A hundred years! Imagine!

Gayev Yes. That is truly something! (*He half embraces it, tender, gentle.*) My dear, honoured bookcase. I salute your life. For one hundred years you have borne witness to the noble ideals of goodness and of justice. For one hundred years your silent call to hard work has sounded in the ears of generation upon generation of this, our family, sustaining us in our moments of weakness, strengthening in us our belief in a better tomorrow, and implanting in us the moral idea of virtue and the moral ideal of social order.

Long pause.

Lopakhin Yes . . .
Mme Ranevsky (*Dry but fond.*) Plus ça change, plus c'est la même chose avec toi, Leon.
Gayev (*A little embarrassed.*) In off into the corner. Cut into the middle.
Lopakhin (*Watch in hand.*) I'll have to go.
Yasha (*Carrying small box on tray.*) I think it's time for your pills.
Pischik Tcha, pills. Never take pills, dear lady. Never did anybody any good. Never did anybody any harm, come to that. Here.

He takes the box, empties the pills into his palm, blows on them, scoops them into his mouth and swallows them with a glass of cider.

See!
Mme Ranevsky (*Surprised, a little alarmed.*) You'll be ill!
Pischik No no. One gulp.

He mimes the action, pleased at the attention.

Nothing.
Lopakhin What guts the man must have.

Laughter.

Firs The honoured gentleman was here at Easter; ate half a bucket of pickled cucumbers. (*Mutters on unintelligibly.*)
Mme Ranevsky What's he saying?
Varya He's muttered for three years. We barely notice it now.
Yasha He's senile.

They look at him, frowning, rather hostile. YASHA *takes a pace back, uncertainly, narrowly missing* CHARLOTTE, *who's just entering behind him, on her way to bed. She's extremely thin, tightly laced, in a white dress with a lorgnette at the waist.*

Lopakhin Ah, forgive me, Charlotte, I haven't had the opportunity to say how do you do yet . . .

He reaches for her hand, to kiss it.

Charlotte (*Withdrawing her hand smartly.*) First the hand, elbow next, then the shoulder . . . Tututut.
Lopakhin Some days it's barely worth getting out of bed! (*Laughter*) Show us a trick then, dear lady.
Mme Ranevsky Excellent idea. Yes.
Charlotte Sorry. Too tired. (*Leaves*)

Lopakhin Well, I'll be away for three weeks. (*Kissing* MME RANEVSKY'S *hand.*) Good-bye, Madame. (*To* GAYEV.) Time to go.

He shakes hands with VARYA; *then, inappropriately, with* FIRS *and* YASHA.

Good-bye.

He walks towards the door, then turns back.

I don't actually feel like going . . . Think about the summer cottage scheme . . . You've only to let me know . . . I'm pretty sure I can raise fifty thousand or so to set things in motion. (*Pause*) Think hard, mm?

Varya (*Angry*) Go, will you. Go!

Lopakhin I'm going, I'm going. (*Leaves*)

GAYEV *follows a few steps towards the door.*

Gayev A perfect boor, that man! Oh, I do beg your pardon, Varya's going to marry him, he's Varya's intended, isn't he . . .

Varya Thank you, Uncle.

Mme Ranevsky No matter, Varya. I shall be more than happy. He's a good man.

Pischik Fine man, admirable fellow, oh yes. My daughter Dashenka says it all the time. My daughter Dashenka says all sorts of things, as a matter of fact.

He nods off at once, snores once, wakes himself up.

While we're on the subject, dear lady, would you lend me two hundred and forty roubles . . . the interest of my mortgage is due tomorrow.

Varya (*Alarmed*) We haven't got it! There isn't any!

Mme Ranevsky I'm afraid that's true. I have nothing.

Pischik Not to worry. (*Laughs*) Never say die, that's the thing. There are times when I think everything's gone, I'm done for. And then, hey presto, there's a railway line or something across my land and I get paid for it! Something will happen, you see; if not today, then tomorrow. I wouldn't be surprised if Dashenka won two hundred thousand roubles in the lottery. She's got a ticket, you know.

Mme Ranevsky So much for coffee. Now I must sleep.

Firs (*Scolding a little, brushing* GAYEV'S *trousers.*) Ach, you've put on the wrong trousers again . . . What am I to do with you!

GAYEV *stands like a statue, barely aware of* FIRS' *fussing.*

Varya (*Low*) Sh. Anya's sleeping. (*Opens window quietly.*) The sun's up. Can you feel it? Look, Mama, the trees. Aren't they wonderful . . . You can smell them on the air. Can you hear the starlings?

GAYEV *detaches from the kneeling* FIRS, *perhaps not noticing him at all, opens another window.*

Gayev How white the orchard, Liuba. Do you remember . . . on and on, the avenue of trees . . . unending . . . shining under the moon like a young maiden's ribbon, ironed and ready for the ball. Remember?

Mme Ranevsky (*Taking the window between them.*) Childhood. And innocence. Oh. (*Long pause, in the hush of the the house.*) My bed was . . . here . . . by the window; I could see the orchard from it. And out there at least, nothing has changed. My orchard gleams as white, as pure as ever, untouched by autumn's storms and winter's dead hand. Here you are again, and again, and again, young, innocent . . . your own self. Some god watches over you. No . . . past to weigh you down like a great stone . . .

Gayev Yes, and odd as it may sound, this same orchard is to be . . .

Mme Ranevsky Look! There's Mother . . . walking through that grove . . . in her white dress! It *is* her! See?

Gayev Where?

Varya (*On her knees, kissing the crucifix on her breast.*) God is with you, Mama.

Mme Ranevsky There's no one. I imagined it. See, over there, on the right, by the path to the summer house, a little white tree, bent over somehow . . . looks like a woman.

Enter TROFIMOV, *very quietly. He's dressed in shabby student's uniform; he's rather bedraggled; wears thick-lensed glasses in wire frames.*

How white and wonderful the blossom against the blue sky . . .

Trofimov Madame Ranevsky.

She turns quickly, startled, stifles a small shriek, stares, recognising him in some part of her mind but unable to acknowledge it.

I just wanted to pay my respects. I'll go. (*He bows formally.*) Forgive me, I was told to wait until the morning, but I still lack patience . . .

Varya (*To* MME RANEVSKY.) It's . . . Peter Trofimov.

Trofimov Peter Trofimov, your son's tutor . . . Can I have changed so much?

MME RANEVSKY *turns quickly back to the window, leaning fractionally on the frame.* GAYEV *puts his hand on her shoulder, uncertain what to do.*

Gayev Come, Liuba, come . . .

Varya I told you wait until tomorrow, Peter . . .

Mme Ranevsky (*In a plain, very normal voice, her back to the room.*) Grisha. Little Grisha.

Varya It was God's will, Mama.

Trofimov I'm sorry. Please.

Mme Ranevsky Was it? To drown a six-year-old child? For what?

She turns into the room, controlled, steady. Holds her hands out, takes TROFIMOV'S.

Do *you* know why it happened, my friend?

She hugs him to her bosom, he begins to greet her more emotionally.

Sh, sh. Anya's sleeping. We mustn't make a noise, mm? (*Standing him away from her.*) Well, Peter. You look terrible. You've grown old.

Trofimov (*Laughing*) A peasant woman in the train called me a 'gentleman gone to seed'.

Mme Ranevsky Then you were just a boy, a pretty young student, and now your hair is thin and you have glasses. What do you do now?

Trofimov I'm still a student. If the authorities have their way, I suspect I'll always be one.

Mme Ranevsky Well. Go to bed now. (*She detaches, kisses* GAYEV.)
You've grown too old, too, Leon. (*She kisses* VARYA, *looks at her, says nothing.*

PISCHIK *begins to follow her out.*

Pischik Ah. Seems to be time for bed. Ooh, this gout. (*Hobbling*) I'll stay the night here, if that's . . . And tomorrow morning, if you could let me have that er two hundred and forty roubles, I'd be of course . . .

Gayev There's no shaking that one.

Pischik . . . most grateful, a mere two hundred and forty roubles, interest on the erm thingumajig . . .

Mme Ranevsky My dear, I have no money.

Pischik Trifling sum. And of course you'd have it back in a, in erm . . .

Mme Ranevsky (*Decisively, from the doorway.*) All right then. Leon will give you the money. Give him the money, Leon.

Gayev Of course. I'll just stand here with my pockets open. (*He does so.*) Come on, help yourself.

Mme Ranevsky What else can we do? He needs it. He'll pay it back.

MME RANEVSKY, TROFIMOV *and* PISCHIK *leave, followed by* FIRS, *losing ground all the time.*

Gayev My sister still knows how to throw money away. Especially mine. (*Sniffing around, locating something. To* YASHA.) Go away. You smell of chickens.

Yasha (*Moving behind him.*) And you, Mr Leon . . . are just the same as ever.

Gayev What did he say? What did he say?

Varya (*To* YASHA.) Your mother's come from the village – she's been sitting in the servants' quarters since yesterday, waiting for you to give her an audience.

Yasha (*Padding out.*) God should have called her long ago.

Varya (*Fierce, crossing herself.*) Have you no shame!

Yasha None at all. She could have come just as well tomorrow.

He leaves. VARYA *begins to clear odd things around the room.* GAYEV *stands for a moment, inside himself, then sits on the sofa carefully, staring at the room as though trying to remember how he got there.*

Varya Mama hasn't changed at all. If it was left to her, she'd give everything we have away.

Gayev Mmm. (*Pause*) Here's what I think: the greater the number of cures you can suggest for a sickness, the more certain you can be it's incurable. I've been rattling my brains a good deal and I've come up with a good many ways out, oh yes, lots and lots . . . so I'm pretty certain we've had it. Anyway, for instance: somebody could leave us some money, that'd be a good thing. Another fine thing would be if Anya were to wed an extremely rich man. And it couldn't hurt for one of us to go to Yaroslavl to try our luck with our old aunt, the countess. Who is, as we all know, exceedingly rich.

Varya (*Overwhelmed, hopeless.*) If only God would see our plight and help us!

Gayev (*A reflex, minimal.*) Don't whine, darling. Now aunt *is* exceedingly rich, but happens not to like us . . . First, because my sister decides to marry some lawyer fellow instead of a nobleman.

ANYA *appears in the doorway, in a white cotton nightgown, like the image of her mother that* LIUBOV *saw in the orchard.* GAYEV *has his back to her.*

. . . So, she marries beneath herself . . . And then she's behaved, erm . . . How can one put it . . . She's not exactly lived the life of a saint. I love her dearly, she's a good, kind . . . impulsive woman, but whatever allowances one cares to make, she has been a trifle what? wanton, mmm? loose, anyway. I mean, my God, it's there every time she moves an eyelash . . .

Varya (*Whispers*) Anya's in the doorway.

Gayev Ach . . . Something in my eye, an eyelash . . . Can't see at all. So . . . Thursday I was at District Council . . .

ANYA *comes into the room.*

Varya You should be sleeping, Anya.

Anya I've tried. I can't.

Gayev (*Kissing* ANYA'*s face and hands.*) Dear, dear girl. Little little girl. (*Weeping*) Niece, angel, everything. Believe me. Please believe me.

Anya Of course I believe you, Uncle. Everyone loves and respects you . . . but you talk too much, Uncle, you should try to keep quiet. What made you say those things about my mother, your sister?

Gayev (*Covering his face with her hand.*) I know, I know, it was awful, it was awful of me. Oh my God, my God! And the speech I made to the bookcase . . . so foolish. It wasn't until I'd finished that I saw how . . . foolish I was being . . .

Varya It's true, your tongue wags, and there you are. Just keep it still, that's all.

Anya It'll make you happier.

Gayev I'll be quiet.

He kisses ANYA'*s and* VARYA'*s hands.*

(*Hands to lips. Silent.*) Nothing. (*He's about to leave.*) Oh, just one thing. I was talking with some friends at the District Council on Thursday and it does look as though it might be possible to raise a loan . . . against promissory notes and so on . . . to at least pay the bank the interest on the erm . . . (*He subsides a moment.*)

Varya May the good Lord help us! (*She mutters a prayer, fearful.*)

Gayev I'm due there again Tuesday and I'll . . . talk some more about it. Do stop whining, Varya. Then, erm, your mother's going to have a talk with Lopakhin: and he'll not refuse her. And when you've rested, you can go to Yaroslavl to see your great-aunt, the countess. And so we'll launch the attack on three fronts and click! it's in the pocket! We'll pay the interest. Sure of it. (*Sweet into mouth. Hand on breast. Sonorous.*) Upon my word of honour, upon anything you like, I swear this estate will not be sold. I hereby solemnly stake my happiness on it! I hereby solemnly give you my hand to it and you can call me a worthless liar if I allow it to come under the hammer. And I do swear all this, by everything I am.

Anya (*Calm now, happier.*) You're a good and clever uncle. (*Puts arm around him.*)

I feel calmer now. Calm and happy.

Enter FIRS.

Firs (*Reproaches him.*) Leon Gayev, to bed! Have you lost all fear of the Almighty One?

Gayev I'm coming, I'm coming. Off you trot, Firs, I can manage by myself, I can undress myself. (FIRS *stands sternly by.*)

Well . . . children . . . time for beddy-byebyes. Further details can wait until tomorrow, but now it's time you were in bed. (*Kisses each in turn*).

Me, I'm an 'eighties man. Those days are out of fashion with most people now, but I've endured much in my life in upholding my beliefs. It's not an accident that I am loved by the peasants hereabouts. Because you have to *know* your peasant. You have to understand his . . .

Anya Again, Uncle?

Varya Listen to it.

Firs (*Sternly*) Mr Gayev.

Gayev Sh! I'm coming! Of course! Go to bed! Off two cushes into the middle, tut, tut, chuc. Pot white, click, chuh.

He leaves. FIRS *totters after him.*

Anya It's so . . . at peace here. I don't want to go to Yaroslavl. I can't stand our great-aunt the countess. Still, I'm at peace here. (*To the doorway.*) Thank you, Uncle.

She sits down, very tired.

Varya I must go to bed. (*Pauses*) You know, a quite nasty thing happened while you were away. The old servants – Efimyushka, Polya, Evstignei, oh and Karp, yes – they started letting vagrants stay in the empty servants' quarters. I didn't say anything at first. Then I heard the gossip they were putting round; that I'd ordered them to be fed on mushy peas and nothing else, because I was *mean*, you see . . . and I heard that all this started with Evstignei . . . so I thought, right, we'll see about this . . . so I sent for him . . . (*She yawns, long and deep. Blinks her eyes.*)

. . . 'So, you silly old man, what's this you've been saying about me . .˙ and stand still when I'm . . .' (*Looks at* ANYA.)

Anya. (ANYA *sleeps.* VARYA *takes her gently by the arm.*)

Come. Sleep in your bed.

She supports ANYA *tenderly towards her bedroom door. In the distance, a shepherd's pipe starts up.* TROFIMOV *comes in, sees* ANYA *on* VARYA'*s arm.*

Varya (*To* TROFIMOV.) Shhh.
Anya (*Half asleep.*) Hear the bells, Varya.
Varya Sh. Sh. Sh. Sh.

They go into ANYA'*s room. Sun floods the nursery now.*

Trofimov Anya. Sun. Spring.

Tape: (TROFIMOV'*s voice*): «Со́лнышко моё!! Весна́ моя!»

ACT II

Black.

Charlotte's voice on tape delivers first line in Russian «У меня нет настóящего пáспорта» etc. Lights up, revealing a stage-wide cyc., dark blue. A guitar strums. A crow barks overhead, once, twice; is answered by another. More lights reveal YASHA *(smoking a long thin cigar), and* DUNYASHA *(powdering her face in a mirror), seated on a crude old country bench:* EPIKHODOV *standing, leg up on a tilted gravestone, playing a love song on a guitar; and* CHARLOTTE, *in hunting clothes and cap, shortening the canvas sling on her rifle. They sit or stand, absorbed, separate, facing out. Behind them, set into the remnant of a wall, a traveller's shrine with a faded blue and gold icon of the Virgin Mary. It's twenty minutes to sunset. A full moon is already faintly silvering their skin.*

Charlotte (*To no one, deep in herself.*) I wonder how old I am. Without papers there's no way of telling. I still think of myself as young, when my father and mother played the fairs and I used to do the death dive into a tub of water. Then they died. A German lady took me in and taught me things. And I grew up. Became a governess. But I have no papers. I could be anybody, from anywhere. I don't even know if my parents were married.

She takes a large cucumber from a jacket pocket, eats it.

I know nothing. If I could talk to someone about it it would help, I know it would. (*Pause*) But there's no one.

Epikhodov (*Sings*)
　　'I've put the world behind me.
　　The world of friend and foe . . .'
　　It is not a thing of beauty, the mandolin . . .

Dunyasha (*Powdering face.*) It's a guitar.

Epikhodov To a man inflamed, it's a mandolin. (*Sings*)
　　If I had your hand to guide me
　　Then true love my soul would know.

Yasha (*Sings*)
　　If I had your hand to guide me
　　I would kiss your little toe.

Charlotte *Ach, mein Gott*, they sing like goats, these people.

Dunyasha (*To* YASHA.) Admit it though. You're very fortunate to have been abroad.

Yasha (*Yawning*) If you like. I agree with you. (*Relights his cigar.*)

Epikhodov I agree too. Abroad they've been a century ahead for years.

Yasha Took the words right out of my mouth.

EPIKHODOV *takes a revolver from his waistband, stares at it for a moment, then places the barrel experimentally in his mouth. Removes it.*

Epikhodov I'm a man of some learning, you know. Oh yes, I've read a good many difficult books, I just can't seem to find my way forward. To be or not to be, really. I should draw your attention here to my habit of always carrying a revolver on my person.

He holds it up. They see it.

Charlotte Right, that's me. (*She slings the rifle over her shoulder.*)

I'm off. Epikhodov, you're clearly a very clever man and I'd wager an extremely dangerous one. Women must be forming lines to fall in love with you. Ha! (*Moves off.*) Oh, the clever ones, the clever ones, I have no one I can talk to, I live alone, I don't know who I am or why I am.

She leaves. YASHA *flicks his cigar, smiling lazily after her.* DUNYASHA *waves the smoke out of her face.* EPIKHODOV *sits on the gravestone, untouched by* CHARLOTTE's *irony.*

Epikhodov I will say this about that. In essence, and without wishing to burk the issues raised, by the way, I feel I should point out that life handles me ruthlessly, as a hurricane might treat a small boat, for instance. Now, in case you imagine I'm mistaken in the matter, explain to me if you can, to take one instance from many, why I should open my eyes this morning and find squatting on my breast a spider of terrifying dimensions... (*He picks up a large stone.*)... like this, mm? Or. Suppose I go to pour a glass of cider, why will the jug inevitably contain some monstrous thing inside it – a cockroach perhaps? Or worse. (*Pause*) Have you read, by chance, the English historian Buckle?

Pause. He crosses to stand behind DUNYASHA, *speaks in her ear.*

May I beg a brief word of you . . . ?
Dunyasha Go on.
Epikhodov Could it be in private, do you think?
Dunyasha (*Discomfited.*) I suppose so. (*She shivers, rubs her upper arms.*)

I shall need my cloak first though. It's by the wardrobe. It's growing quite cold out here . . .
Epikhodov As you wish, Madame. (*Collects his guitar, begins to leave.*) I think I know now what I should do with my revolver. (*Leaves*)
Yasha (*Yawning. Finally.*) Treat this as a confidence, won't you, but that man is very stupid.
Dunyasha Please God he doesn't shoot himself. (*Checks her image in the mirror, angles it to take in* YASHA.)

These days I'm nervy all the time, worrying. I've worked at the big house since I was a child, see. My hands are as fair as any lady's, I don't know how to live ordinarily any more. See. (*She holds her hands out.*)

I've grown so soft and delicate that the least thing sets me off trembling . . . the least thing. (*Turns to face him.*) I mean, Yasha, if you play me false, I'll break into tiny pieces, I know I will . . .

Yasha (*Kissing her hands.*) Sh, little cucumber. Sh. (*Calms her.*) A girl must know her station, of course. In my view, there's nothing less endearing than a girl who doesn't know how to behave well.

Dunyasha But I love you, Yasha. Terribly. You're so . . . cultured, you can talk about anything . . .

Yasha (*Yawning*) Yes, I know. And yet, see it my way, child: a girl who loves is a girl who sins, isn't that so. (*Shifts, looks around, lounges back a little on the bench.*)

Is there anything more luxurious than smoking a cigar outdoors. (*Listens*) Christ, there's someone coming . . . it's the gentry.

He lobs the cigar away at once, goes to stand up and fasten his jacket, is thwarted by DUNYASHA, *who has knelt between his legs and is now clinging to them, whispering,* 'Your word, Yasha, your word.' YASHA *swipes the cigar smoke away as best he can.*

You'd best go on back. Quickly. (*Drawing her up.*) Here. (*He picks up a bottle of wine, pours some over her head.*)

Look as if you've been swimming in the river or something. Not that way, *that* way . . . I don't want them thinking I've been making assignations . . .

Dunyasha (*Coughing*) My head's reeling. I think it's your cigar. (*Leaves*)

YASHA *crosses to the shrine, sits.* MME RANEVSKY *and* GAYEV *are heard approaching for quite a while, then seen, arm in arm, cresting the bank.* MME RANEVSKY *sings a French love song (perhaps Bizet),* GAYEV *tum-tums a rhythm out. Behind then comes* LOPAKHIN, *his jacket over his arm. We hear his opening line before we see him.*

Lopakhin I need a decision – time is not on your side. It's a simple enough question: will you agree to lease the land for weekend cottages or not? One word will do: yes or no.

They sway a little, still slightly fumed from luncheon wine.

Mme Ranevsky Somebody's been smoking cigars. Filthy things.

She sits on the bench, ignoring YASHA.

Gayev See, Liuba, it's over there. (*She follows his finger, frowning.*)

The railway. (*She nods.*)

Very convenient. (*To* LOPAKHIN.) We've been to town for lunch . . . Yellow in the . . . middle, I think. (*He gestures the nomination.*) I think I'd like to go off and have a quick frame . . .

Mme Ranevsky No hurry.

Lopakhin Just one tiny word, mm?

Gayev What?

Mme Ranevsky (*Rummaging in her purse.*) All gone. Yesterday it was full to here. My poor Varya skimps and saves and feeds the servants mushy peas and milk soup and here am I throwing it away on nothing . . . (*She drops the purse; her remaining gold coins scatter around her feet.*) See. Just look at me. (*She laughs suddenly, unamusedly.*)

Yasha Allow me.

He kneels before her, begins gathering the coins from under the bench, brushing her feet and ankles with his hands.

Mme Ranevsky Thank you, Yasha . . . (GAYEV *sits by her, pats her hand.*)

Oh why in God's name did I go out to lunch? That dismal restaurant of yours, Leon, with its ageing trio in the corner and the tablecloths smelling of the laundry. Need we drink so much? Or eat? Or talk? Today, Leon, you talked everyone to the point of physical extinction, and about what? Trivia. Irrelevancies. The seventies, for God's sake. The Decadents. And to whom? (*To* LOPAKHIN.) Fancy talking to *waiters* about poets!

Lopakhin Quite.

YASHA *begins to reach for a coin between* GAYEV'*s feet.*

Gayev Yes, I'm quite beyond redemption, I can see that . . . (*To* YASHA.) What are you worming around at, eh?

Yasha (*Half sotto, directed with care and precision.*) Trying not to laugh at *you.*

Gayev (*Stands dramatically.*) It's him or me, Liuba . . .

Mme Ranevsky (*Casual, dismissive, kicks* YASHA *on the hip.*) Out. Go. Allez-vous en.

Yasha (*Standing, giving her the purse.*) At once, Madame. (*He bows low.*) Il faut!

He leaves slowly, clicking something in his hand, laughing a little, not quite discreetly, something in his manner suggesting a secret shared with MME RANEVSKY *that will protect him.*

LOPAKHIN *watches him leave. He homes in deliberately on* RANEVSKY.

Lopakhin So. Deriganov intends spending a fraction of his fortune on buying your estate. They say he'll attend the auction in person.

Mme Ranevsky Who says so?

Lopakhin It's what they say in town.

Gayev There's money promised from Yaroslavl, our aunt, you know, but when and how much of it, ppp, nobody knows . . .

Lopakhin (*Ignores him.*) Will she send a hundred thousand, two hundred thousand, what do you think?

Mme Ranevsky Well, let me see, if we're very lucky it could be as much as fifteen.

Lopakhin Thousand. (*She nods, smiles.*)

I'm trying not to give offence, but you two must be just about the most reckless and feckless people I've ever met. You're told in words of one syllable – you are about to lose your land – and it seems to make no impression.

Mme Ranevsky (*Teasing, tipsy still.*) But what can we *do* about it? Have *you* an answer?

Lopakhin (*Blowing a little, seeking and quickly finding his self-control.*) I give you the answer every single day, there *is* only one answer: the orchard and the land down to the river must be leased out for summer cottages. And it must be done *now*, the auction's almost upon us. Do you *understand*?

He looks from one to the other. MME RANEVSKY *has removed a shoe to stroke the arch of her foot.* GAYEV *chalks his cue with languid precision.*

When you make *that* decision, you'll get the credit you need and you'll be saved.

Ranevsky Summer cottages, weekenders—it's all so 'bourgeois'.

Gayev Absolutely.

Lopakhin You know something, you people would make a saint lose his temper, or burst into tears or something. (*Looks at* GAYEV.) And you, you're driving *me* mad, you old woman you.

Gayev Old what did he say?

Lopakhin (*Shouts*) Woman. Old *woman*!

He prepares to leave, grim, disturbed, and somehow resolute.

Mme Ranevsky (*Standing*) Don't go. Please. Dear man. Please. Perhaps. we can think of something . . . together.

Lopakhin I doubt it.

Mme Ranevsky Please. (LOPAKHIN *walks in looping circles, charmed into indirection yet trying to stay firm.*) I beg of you. It's always so much cheerier when you're with us. (*Pause. She watches him carefully.*)

I beg of you. It's always so much cheerier when you're with us.

Pause. She watches him carefully.

I'm terrified something will happen – the house fall down around us, or worse.

Gayev Double into the middle there, spot into the top . . .

Lopakhin How do you mean?

Mme Ranevsky We have committed many sins.

Lopakhin You?

Gayev Sins? Oh yes. (*Puts a sweet in his mouth.*) They say I've sucked a fortune away in sweeties. (*He laughs.*)

Mme Ranevsky (*Taking* LOPAKHIN's *fixed gaze.*) Yes. A great many. I've thrown money away all my life, like someone mad, and I chose a husband whose only talent lay in the creation of debts. Oh and drinking – he was a fairly active drunkard – died eventually of a surfeit of champagne. And what do I do? I fall in love with his double. And while we're having our affair, I receive my first punishment, like a bullet here, here . . . (*She places a hand on her breast, the brittleness falling away in the silence.*)

. . . my first born drowns, here, in the river. (*Pause*)

I went abroad, away for good, I swore I'd never look at this river again, I shut my eyes to all responsibilities, grief makes one cruel you know, and ran away. He followed me, this second brutal man, fell ill in Menton and forced me to buy a house there and nurse him. For three years I slaved over him, day and night, until he . . . wore me out and my soul withered. (*Pause*) A year ago I sold the house to pay off our debts and fled to Paris. Where he robbed me, threw me over and took up with someone else. I tried poisoning myself . . . I couldn't bear the shame . . . it was all so futile suddenly. (*She's weeping, barely aware of it; wipes her face with the heel of her hand.*)

And just as suddenly, I longed to be in Russia again, home again, with my little girl again. May the Lord have mercy on me and forgive me my trespasses and let the punishment come to an end. (*She takes out a handkerchief to wipe her face, draws out a telegram with it.*)

This came today from Paris . . . He wants me back, asks my forgiveness . . . (*She tears it up slowly but without malice.*)

Is that music I can hear?

They listen. We hear nothing.

Gayev It's probably our famous Jewish orchestra. Remember? Three violins, flute, double bass?

Mme Ranevsky Are they still going? We should have them to the house sometime and arrange a ball or something.

Lopakhin (*Still listening.*) Don't hear it. (*Sings*)
    For a schilling the kraut
    Turns a bear inside out
    Until he can dance like a frog.
(*Laughs*) I saw an excellent piece at the theatre yesterday. Very very funny.

Mme Ranevsky I'm sure it wasn't in the least funny. (*Pause*) I believe people like you would do better examining their own lives instead of going to the theatre to observe others'. Don't you sense how vapid your life is and how silly your attempts to explain it.

Lopakhin I suppose it's true. Looked at rationally life *is* pretty meaningless. (*Pause*) Look at me and my father. He was a peasant, a clod, incapable of learning anything or of handing anything on to me by way of wisdom. The closest we ever got was when he'd come home drunk and thrash me with a stick. (*Pause*)

So: am I any different? I'm scarcely less mindless than him, I've learned next to nothing, my handwriting's . . . I write like a pig . . . I'm ashamed to let it be seen.

Long pause. LOPAKHIN *kicks at a stone bedded in the earth.* GAYEV *stares at the moon, his face almost lost behind him.*

Mme Ranevsky (*Soft, gentle.*) You need a wife, old friend.
Lopakhin Yes.
Mme Ranevsky You should marry my Varya. She's a good girl.
Lopakhin Yes.
Mme Ranevsky (*Slow, distinct, simple.*) She comes from sturdy, common stock, works the clock round, and loves you. You've been fond of her for a long time, am I right?
Lopakhin I wouldn't say no, I suppose. She's a good girl.

Pause. They're on the delicate brink of something.

Gayev I've been offered a position at the bank, six thousand a year, did I tell you?
Mme Ranevsky (*The moment blown for her: angered into coldness and contempt.*) What, you? You just stay here . . .

FIRS *mumbles his way over the knoll, an overcoat in his arms.*

Firs Be so kind as to put this on, sir. You'll take a chill.
Gayev (*Snatches it from him, puts it on.*) You begin to annoy me, my man.
Firs Exactly. Off you go this morning and not a word to me. (*Inspects him minutely.*)
Mme Ranevsky You've grown old, Firs.
Firs What can I bring you, Madam?
Lopakhin The mistress said you've grown old.
Firs It's all the years I've been alive, that's what it is. They were trying to marry *me* off before your father was born. (*Laughs*) And by the time we got our freedom, I was already principal valet. So I refused to take it, the freedom, and stayed with the master and the mistress . . . (*Thinks, laughing a little still.*) I remember the celebrations when the freedom came. (*Thinks on.*) Everyone so happy and no one knowing what there was to be glad about.
Lopakhin Ah, those good old days, when you could depend on things . . . Getting flogged, for example.
Firs (*Deep in himself.*) Precisely. The serfs belonged to their masters and the masters owned the serfs. Now it is all so messy and you can't make sense of any of it.

Gayev (*A bark.*) Firs!

> FIRS *turns to look at him.*

> (*Distinctly*) Shut up. (*Pause*)

> Tomorrow I go to town. I'm told there's a certain general who's prepared to advance me a loan against my signature.

Lopakhin I shouldn't bother. You couldn't raise the interest on the loan you'll need . . .

Mme Ranevsky He's daydreaming. There is no general.

> ANYA *and* VARYA *arrive, arm in arm.*

Gayev Ah, the children.

Anya (*To* VARYA.) *There's* mother.

> TROFIMOV *has followed them on, some paces behind.*

Mme Ranevsky Come, come my darlings. (*She kisses each in turn.*)

> I love you both very much. Here – (*she pats the bench*) – sit here beside me.

> *They join her on the bench.*

Lopakhin (*Sees* TROFIMOV.) Aha. The 'everlasting undergraduate' is never very far from the ladies.

Trofimov So? What's that to you?

Lopakhin Fifty next birthday and still no degree.

Trofimov You have the wit of a polar bear, Lopakhin.

Lopakhin Easy, boy, easy. Just joking.

Trofimov So don't. All right?

Lopakhin (*Laughs*) One question, then, and I'll leave you alone. (TROFIMOV *doesn't dissent.*)

> What do you think of me?

> *Small silence. The others watch.*

Trofimov (*Finally*) Well, I think of you this way, Alex: you're rich already and nothing will stop you getting richer; in the larger perspective, based upon the scientific laws of nature, I'd say you were 'necessary' in exactly the way that a wild animal that must eat its prey is necessary.

> *Laughter, though not too much from* LOPAKHIN.

Varya You're better on astral bodies, Peter.

Mme Ranevsky No, I want to go on with yesterday's subject.

Trofimov What was that?

Gayev Pride, wasn't it?

Trofimov We talked about many things and agreed on none of them. (*Settling* *himself.*) All right. You people talk about 'the proud man' as though the concept were in some way importantly mystical. It's possible you're right, for yourselves anyway. Yet if we choose to look at it in basic terms and avoid sophisticated complications, we *have* to ask: what has man to be proud *about*? When most men on earth are physically underdeveloped, intellectually retarded and emotionally profoundly miserable, what right have we to be proud? It's time we stopped praising our species and got down to *work*. There's nothing else.

Gayev Does it matter what we do? We all die in the end.

Trofimov Do we? What does it mean: to die? Suppose man to have . . . a hundred senses and five of them – the five we know – are lost to us in death, while the rest live on . . .

Mme Ranevsky What a clever thought, Peter.

Lopakhin (*Ironic*) Brilliant, Peter.

Trofimov Man *can* make progress, struggle for perfection. There *is* a discernible future in which we'll find solutions to the problems that confront us now; but we'll achieve it only through unremitting struggle, by working with all our strength to help those who are even now seeking the answers. Here, now, in Russia, very few are embarked on that course. The greater part of the intelligentsia seek nothing, do nothing and appear congenitally incapable of work of any kind. They bask in the term 'intelligentsia' and treat their servants like an inferior species and peasants like beasts of burden. Their scholarship is banal, their level of culture nil, their grasp of science non-existent and their feeling for art trivial and irrelevant. Of course, they can look as grave as anyone and talk about important matters and make metaphysical speculations with the best, while all around them, right beneath their eyes, the workers eat scraps of rancid meat and sleep on bare boards thirty or forty to a room. Bedbugs, shit, leaking roofs, moral degradation. And then it becomes obvious that all our 'philosophical' salon chat has only one purpose: namely, to distract ourselves *and everyone else* in society from the real issues. What happened to all those creches we talked about so far into the night, year after year, those libraries, those workers' housing schemes? You'll find them in novels; they don't actually exist. What we have achieved is widespread misery, bourgeois vulgarity and moral barbarism. (*Pause*)

I fear those 'grave' faces we pull, these 'earnest' discussions we endlessly embark on. Fear them and despise them. We'd do better to hold our tongues.

Silence. TROFIMOV *walks away towards the knoll, the anger still working.* LOPAKHIN *follows him a few paces, looks back at the seated group.*

Lopakhin (*Quietly*) I speak only for myself. I'm up before five every day and I work from morning to night. I handle a good deal of money, my own and others', so I get a chance to meet people and see what they're like. Only through working can one appreciate how few honest and honourable people there are. (*Pause, as he searches.*)

There are nights I lie awake, trying to make sense of it all; and I think ... God, you have given us endless forests, endless fields, endless horizons ... why are we not *giants*, in such a place as this ...?

Mme Ranevsky Giants? (*Long pause.*)

Giants are for fairy tales. In life they're always terrifying.

EPIKHODOV *crosses the skyline, strumming a sad tune.*

Mme Ranevsky Epikhodov ...
Anya Epikhodov ...
Gayev Exit the sun, my friends.
Trofimov Exit the sun.
Gayev (*Quiet, as though reciting.*) Nature, so glorious, burning with undying fires, so fair and yet so unfeeling, you, whom we call mother, fusing in your core both life and death, making gifts of both indifferently ...
Varya Uncle!
Anya Not again, Uncle, please ...
Trofimov (*Gently*) Try the red into the middle.
Gayev I'm quiet. (*Fingers to lips.*) Nothing.

They sit or stand in silence, save for FIRS's *muttering. Suddenly a sound is heard, far off, yet fractionally closer than before (Act I). The sound of a string snapping and dying away.*

Mme Ranevsky What was it?
Lopakhin I don't know. It sounded like a cable snapping in a mineshaft a long way away.
Gayev Perhaps it was a bird. It could've been a heron.
Trofimov Or an owl.
Mme Ranevsky (*Trembles a little.*) Something ... unpleasant ...

Silence.

Firs It's happened before. Just before the misfortune. An owl hooted. (*Pause*) And the samovar coughed.
Gayev Before what misfortune?
Firs Before they set us free.

Silence.

Mme Ranevsky (*Standing*) We should go, my friends. It's almost night. (*To* ANYA.) You're crying ... what is it, my love? (*Draws* ANYA *to her.*)
Anya Nothing. It's nothing.
Trofimov We have company.

A man appears, youngish, in a battered military hat and greatcoat. He weaves a little on his approach. The group defines itself against him.

Man Would you know if there's a way through to the station from here?

Gayev There is indeed. That road there.

Man Greatly beholden . . . (*Begins to cough, at first almost comically, but it uglily persists.*)

Handsome weather . . . handsome. (*Half shouts.*) 'Brothers, starving and suffering comrades, unite now by the river, let them *hear* your misery . . .' (*To* VARYA, *very suddenly.*) Mamselle, a starving Russian asks you for thirty kopeks . . .

VARYA *yelps, frightened, pulls away from him.*

Lopakhin (*Stepping forward, angry.*) You'd do better learning a few manners . . .

The man gives no ground. LOPAKHIN *advances no further.*

Mme Ranevsky You. (*The man looks at her.*)

Here, take this.

She has her purse open, fiddles for a coin.

I have no silver . . . here, here's a gold one.

The man takes it carefully, studies it and then the group.

Man (*Bows, ironically.*) Greatly beholden, I'm sure.

He leaves in a long, winding movement, laughing to himself. They watch him off; a small laugh spreading and growing among them when he's finally gone.

Varya (*Still trembling.*) I'm going back. Oh Mother, how could you, what am I to feed the servants with . . . ?

Mme Ranevsky (*The irony harshening, as the wine sours.*) There's nothing to be done with a fool like me, eh? I'll give you everything I have when we get back. Lopakhin: let me have some more money please.

Lopakhin A pleasure.

Mme Ranevsky Come along, it's time we went. (*They gather themselves around her to depart.*)

Oh by the way, Varya, we've just been arranging your wedding! My warmest congratulations.

Varya (*Hurt, low voice.*) It's sad you find that so . . . amusing, Mama . . .

Lopakhin Euphemia, get thee to a monastery.

Gayev See my hands . . . itching for the cue.

Lopakhin (*In* VARYA's *ear.*) Euphemia, sprite, remember me in your horizons.

Mme Ranevsky We must go. It's almost time for dinner . . .

Varya What a dreadful man. My heart's still pounding.

They leave en bloc, with no particular haste. LOPAKHIN *strides after them, calling after them as he goes, leaving* ANYA *and* TROFIMOV *together.*

Lopakhin I trust nobody needs reminding that orchard and estate come under the auctioneer's hammer in two weeks' time . . . Two weeks, friends. Try to think of it a little, while you dine . . .

He leaves.

ANYA *has followed the group a little before turning back to* TROVIMOV. *She watches him as he crosses to the bench, sits on its back, his feet on the seat, staring out. She laughs. He looks at her briefly.*

Anya It was good of our travelling friend to scare dear Varya. (*Pause*) It means we can be alone.

Trofimov Varya's scared by most things. For days on end she's trailed us, scared we're going to suddenly fall in love. She can't get it into her narrow bourgeois head that we've no use for it, this 'falling in love'. (*He stands on the bench, strides in a little, an orator of sorts.*)

We have one goal and one meaning for our lives: to throw off the shackles of the metaphysical and the second-hand and everything else that makes us unfree and unhappy. Forward, mes amis, meine Kameraden. We're on the march towards the brightest star in all history . . . (*He stops, smiles a little at* ANYA*'s rapt, silvered face below him.*)

. . . the one over there, see it? (*She nods vigorously.*)

So forward! No faltering now.

He laughs, exhilarated. ANYA *claps her hands, part of his vast audience.*

Anya Bravo, Monsieur! I love your words, I love them.

He gets down from the bench, approaches her, stares at her a long moment. She hesitates, perhaps not knowing what will happen.

Isn't it . . . wonderful here . . . today . . . ?

Trofimov (*Dry, still staring at her face.*) Yes. Perfect weather.

Anya You've done something to me, Peter. (*His face gestures the question.*)

Something. (*She detaches, walks behind the bench, turns to look at him.*)

Why do I . . . care less about the cherry orchard than I used to? I loved it once like a . . . like a person, family, there was nothing dearer in the world than our orchard.

Trofimov Because. Our orchard is all of Russia. Mmm? This vast, amazing continent, think of all the fine places there are in it. (*Pause*)

And think of something else, Anya: your father's father, and his father, and his, were owners of serfs. They owned human lives, Anya. From every tree in your orchard there are people hanging, they peer at you through the branches, you can hear their voices moaning in the leaves . . . Owning other human beings is what has destroyed your line – those who came before, those who live on – so that your mother, your uncle, you yourself still can't quite grasp that you're living and always have lived off the sweat and labour of someone else, off those same people you wouldn't allow across your back doorstep. Don't you see, Anya, we're still living two hundred years back somewhere, we haven't understood our own history. Instead, we gravely talk, bewail our boredom and drink ourselves stupid. (*Pause*)

When we can expiate the past, redeem our history, we can put a match to it for good and begin living in the present. But we can redeem ourselves only by struggle, only by hard and attritional effort. It's *this* you must understand, little one.

Anya (*Low, intense.*) I shall leave that house – it has never been ours – I give you my word.

Trofimov Throw the keys in the well and go, free as air.

Anya Free as air. Yes.

Trofimov And here's *my* word, Anya. Being a student and still relatively young hasn't protected me from hard times. Come winter, I'm forced to scrounge for food, I fall ill and I'm never sure I'll see another spring. And life drives *me* before it as it does the really poor, the truly oppressed. And yet – you have my word for it, Anya – there is not a moment passes that my spirit does not teem with the marvellous possibilities of this species. There is . . . such joy to come, Anya: I can see it.

Silence.

Anya (*Finally*) See, Peter. The moon.

EPIKHODOV's *guitar can be heard, slow, sad. The moon has risen.* VARYA *calls, 'Anya. Anya,' somewhere else.*

Trofimov (*Softly*) Varya. Will she never stop!

Anya (*Gently*) It doesn't matter. Let's go to the river. It'll be good there.

Trofimov Yes.

They leave. VARYA *calls on, on tape, in Russian:* «Аня! Аня!»

ACT III

Black.

A double bass bows a slow, menacing rhythm; in time, a flute lays down a funereal melody; a violin eventually joins it with harmony.

Half lights up on the ballroom, seen through an arch and through thick, semi-transparent gauze drapes that constitute the dividing wall, on each side of it, between ballroom and drawing-room.

Five men and five women, variously masked, stand in a line facing out, men left, women right. PISCHIK's *voice is heard on tape:* 'Promenade à une paire.' *The men select their partners, the remaining violins augment the funereal 'rond' and a slow circular promenade begins.*

PISCHIK, *one of the dancers, calls:* 'Grand rond, balancez.' *Ballroom and drawing-room lights to full; the dance picks up.*

PISCHIK *and* CHARLOTTE, *the leading pair, draw the dance down the two steps beneath the chandeliered archway and into the drawing-room (where furniture has been relocated around a dancing circle in the centre).* TROFIMOV *and* RANEVSKY, ANYA *and the post office clerk,* VARYA *and the stationmaster follow. As they clear the ballroom, we see the five-man Jewish band, bearded to a man, on the ballroom's far wall.* DUNYASHA *and her partner bring up the rear. As* PISCHIK *leads the pairs back into the ballroom,* FIRS *enters the drawing-room from the hall. He wears a tail coat and carries a tray of mineral water.* PISCHIK *calls, 'Les cavaliers à genoux et remerciez vos dames,' to signal the end of the rond; the men kneel and kiss the women's gloves.* FIRS *places the tray on a table, begins his slow rattle off again.* PISCHIK *and* TROFIMOV, *pushing masks on to foreheads, come down into the drawing-room, as the others break into talking groups beyond.*

Pischik Too much blood, that's my trouble. Had a couple of strokes already, makes dancing hard for me, but you know what they say, if you run with the pack you've got to waggle your tail whether you've teeth left or not. Actually, I've got the strength of a horse. My dear departed father always claimed the Pischiks were direct descendants of the very horse the Emperor Caligula installed in the Roman Senate – father always loved a joke, God bless him. (*He sits on a deep chair.*)

Trouble is, I've no money. And a hungry horse can only think of feed . . . (*Settles a little, eyes closed, snores; snorts awake.*) Me too: only with me it's money . . .

Trofimov (*Studying him; ironic.*) You know, Simon, there *is* something of the horse about you . . .

People are playing billiards in the billiard room to the right; VARYA *appears on the steps beneath the connecting arch.*

Trofimov (*Seeing her; teasing.*) Ah, it's Madame Lopakhin.

Varya (*Steely*) Ah, the gentleman gone to seed.

Trofimov (*Bowing*) Gone to seed and proud of it, Ma'am.

Varya (*Leaving; bitter.*) Now we have an orchestra . . . Pity nobody thought about paying for it . . .

Trofimov (*To* PISCHIK.) You know, if all the energy we directed towards 'finding the money' and 'paying for it' had been put to some other end, we could have . . . re-made the universe by now.

Pischik Do you know Nietzsche says – the philosopher, you know, great man, very famous, first-class intellect – he says . . . somewhere . . . one has the right to forge banknotes?

Trofimov You've read Nietzsche then?

Pischik No, not exactly. Dashenka told me . . . about it. But at the moment I'm in such a mess I might be forced to follow his advice, I can tell you. I've got to find three hundred and ten roubles for the day after tomorrow, and so far I've managed a mere hundred and thirty . . . (*Pats his pocket, to indicate them; feels nothing.*)

Oh my God, I've lost it, it's not there, I've lost the money. (*Hands feverish around other pockets.*)

Sweet Jesus, where's the money . . . (*Shout of relief, as he locates it.*)

Aaah! It's here! Inside the lining! Look at me, I'm sweating. Oh.

MME RANEVSKY *and* CHARLOTTE *come in,* MME RANEVSKY *singing a rough, spry Caucasian dance tune* (*Legzinka*).

Mme Ranevsky What's keeping Leon? What's he doing in town anyway? (*To* DUNYASHA, *mooning by.*) Tea for the musicians, Dunyasha. Tea.

Trofimov It's possible the auction didn't even get off the ground.

Mme Ranevsky It's all so . . . inappropriate. Hiring musicians. Giving a ball. Ah well . . .

She sits, rather heavily; tired; hums the legzinka a moment, but as fragments, slow tempo, lifelessly.

CHARLOTTE *still masked; top hat, checked trousers; gives* PISCHIK *a pack of cards.*

Charlotte Here. Now think of a card.

Pischik Done. (*Thinks*) I've thought.

Charlotte Right, shuffle. Sehr gut. Now . . . hand it to me, sweet Pischik. Ein, zwei, drei. And . . . look in your side pocket there . . .

Pischik (*Producing it.*) Well I'm damned, the eight of spades! Just imagine!

Charlotte (*Palming deck; to* TOFIMOV.) Top card, name it. Quick!

Trofimov Erm . . . Queen of Spades.

Charlotte (*Showing it, casual*) Parfait! (*To* PISCHIK.) And you. Go!

Pischik Ace of Hearts.

Charlotte (*Showing it.*) Just so! (*Claps hands, cards disappear.*) Beautiful weather we're having. (*A mysterious feminine voice from under the floor boards*) 'Yes indeed, beautiful, Madame.'

You're a very charming beau, you know. (*Voice*) 'And I have the highest regard for you, Madame.'

Stationmaster (*Who's approached through the arch during the performance.*) Bravo, Madame ventriloquist!

Pischik Never saw anything like it! Mamselle Charlotte, you're ravishing . . . I could eat you . . .

Charlotte Really? You wouldn't know where to begin. 'A good enough man, but a lousy musician.'

Trofimov Never mind, old horse.

Charlotte Attention, please. One more.

She whisks a knee rug from a chair. People filter down from the ballroom to watch.

This very fine rug for sale, what am I offered now, who'll start the bidding?

Pischik Did you ever see anything like it!

Charlotte Ein, zwei, drei!

Whips the rug away, to reveal ANYA *standing behind it.* ANYA *curtseys, runs to her mother, kisses her, retires to the ballroom to applause.*

Mme Ranevsky Bravo, bravo.

Charlotte One more. Ein, zwei, drei.

VARYA *appears, bows.*

Pischik She's done it again, the little devil!

Charlotte Fin! C'est tout!

She flings the rug over PISCHIK, *curtseys, runs into the ballroom.* PISCHIK *gallomphs after her, struggling with the rug, lusting visibly.*

Pischik (*Leaving*) What about that then, eh? The little vixen, let me at her . . .

People filter off, leaving MME RANEVSKY, VARYA *and* TROFIMOV *in the drawing-room.* MME RANEVSKY *looks at* VARYA, *who shakes her head: no word.*

Mme Ranevsky Still no sign of Leon. I can't imagine what he's found to do in town that could keep him so long. Either the estate's been sold or it hasn't – why keep us in ignorance?

Varya Uncle will have bought it, I'm sure of it.

Trofimov Oh, of course.

Varya (*Sparking a little at his sarcasm.*) Great aunt has authorised uncle to buy it in her name and transfer the debt. She's doing it for Anya. And I'm sure God would not have it otherwise – uncle will have bought it.

Mme Ranevsky (*Cutting across the rhetoric.*) Our good great aunt in Yaroslavl has sent fifteen thousand roubles – not even enough to cover the interest, let alone purchase the estate, in her or anyone else's name . . . (*Covers face with hands. Uncovers it.*) It's my life they're handling down there. My life.

Trofimov (*Whisper*) Madame Lopakhin.

Varya (*Angry whisper.*) Everlasting undergraduate. Who ever heard of being expelled *twice*!

Mme Ranevsky Varya! Stop spitting, girl. So he teases you about Lopakhin, why should it matter? If you like Lopakhin, marry him and be done with it. He's a decent man, not without . . . interest. If you don't want to, don't. Nobody's forcing you, child.

Varya I know that, Mother. It's just not something I can . . . joke about. (*Pause*) He *is* a good man . . . and I do have . . . feelings for him . . .

Mme Ranevsky So marry him. I don't understand what you're waiting for.

Varya Mother, I can't do it on my *own*, can I? For two years it's been in the air, everybody's talked about it. But he says nothing. Or jokes. And I can see why. He's busy . . . building, getting rich: there's no time for me. (*Pause*)

If I had any money at all, a . . . hundred roubles would do, I'd leave it all, everything and everyone, I'd find a convent at the other end of the country . . .

Trofimov Ah, and such *peace* you'd find there!

Varya Our undergraduate must have his wit, must'nt he. (*Soft, regret and pity staining the voice.*) You've grown so . . . ugly, Peter. So old. (*Gathering; to* MME RANEVSKY.) I need to be *working*, Mother. I need to be doing things . . .

YASHA *comes in, poorly suppressing a giggling fit.*

Yasha (*Affecting solemnity at last, as though announcing a guest.*) Epikhodov has broken a billiard cue.

He leaves.

Varya (*Huge frustration.*) Why is Epikhodov even *here*? And who gave him per*miss*ion to play billiards? I don't understand these . . . people . . .

She leaves.

Mme Ranevsky (*Gently*) Don't tease her, Peter. She's unhappy enough as it is, without that.

Trofimov (*Roaming a little.*) She's so officious, Liuba. She . . . interferes in everything. She's plagued Anya and me all summer long, looking to nip some hypothetical romance in the bud. (*Pause*)

It's none of her business. (*Pause*)

Besides which, it's bloody insulting; I'm above that sort of crass senti-mentalism . . . we're *both* above it, as a matter of fact.

Mme Ranevsky (*Standing*) Meaning I'm below it, I suppose. (*He begins to protest her interpretation, she gestures him not to.*)

Where's Leon! All I want to know is: have I been sold or not? I suppose all . . . disasters are incomprehensible; I don't know what to think, I seem . . . lost somehow. I feel like screaming or something even more banal and stupid. (*Turning to* TROFIMOV.) Help me. Say something. Please.

She's distraught, under the effort of control. TROFIMOV *takes her by the arm, restores her to her chair, squats beside her.*

Trofimov (*Distinctly*) Liuba. It doesn't matter. Sold or not sold, it has no meaning now. That's all in the past; finished with long ago. The fields have reclaimed the thin road you travelled. Be easy now. Eschew . . . self-deceptions. For perhaps the first time in your life, you're allowed to stare truth frankly in the face.

Mme Ranevsky Truth? What's that? Perhaps you can see it, your eyes are young. *I* look and I see nothing. Such confidence you have, Peter – is there a problem in the world you can't solve? But think about it: isn't it only that none of the problems you solve has ever really touched you; hurt you. When you look so . . . bravely to the future, isn't it only that you haven't had the experience to make you fearful. You're braver, deeper, honester than any of us, but you lack . . . generosity, you lack consideration. Just think a little more about *us*, Peter, just a little, mm? I was born here, and my father, and his father before him. I love it, this place, house, orchard; without them, there's no meaning to my life. I'd sooner be sold *with* them than left without them.

She takes TROFIMOV's *head in her hands, kisses him on the forehead.*

It's where my son was drowned. Here. Give me *some* pity, dear, loving friend.

Trofimov I sympathise deeply, you know that.

Mme Ranevsky (*Pushing him away rather violently.*) Then why can't you say it *differently*? Differently! (*She rips a handkerchief from her pocket; a telegram falls to the floor.*)

Do you have any idea how things like this . . . drag one down? Like millstones. (*Noisy laughter erupts in the ballroom.*)

Listen to them . . . They make noise and know nothing and every sound they make puts a drill to my soul. Look, see me trembling . . . but I can't go to my room. Because the silence frightens me more. (*Pause. She holds her hand out for his, draws him back to the chair.*)

So don't judge me, Peter, you're like a son to me. Marry Anya if you will, you have my blessing, only you must get down to your studies and graduate. What do you actually do, eh? Nothing. Life drives you along like the rest of us – (*stroking his hair now*) – isn't that odd, mm? N'est-ce pas, cheri? (*Laughs*) And you'll just have to do something with this beard, it's so piffling. What a funny boy you are.

Trofimov (*Picking up the telegram; nettled.*) I have no wish to be a beau, Mme Ranevsky.

Mme Ranevsky It's from Paris. They come every day. That . . . farouche man is ill again, he's 'up against it' again . . . He wants me to forgive him and . . . go back to Paris. And I think I should go and be with him for a time. Don't frown, Peter, what else can I do, darling, what else is there? He's on his own; sick; miserable; who'll look after him, keep him sane, wash his face and hands and give him his pills if I don't? I love him. (*Pause. She watches him.*)

Without shame, without fear: *love* him. Isn't it obvious? He's like a great stone round my neck and it'll drag me to the bottom with him . . . but it's a stone I love and can't live without. (TROFIMOV *goes to say something.*)

Don't *judge* me, Peter, all right? Don't say anything. Don't talk at all.

Trofimov (*Upset; angry at his overt emotion.*) By God, I will though, and you'll have to forgive my candour, but that . . . man has . . . robbed you, over and over . . .

Mme Ranevsky (*Covering her ears.*) . . . That's enough. I'll hear no more of that talk . . .

Trofimov . . . That man is a pig and everyone knows it save you. A scrounger, a grubby nothing . . .

Mme Ranevsky . . . Peter, you're twenty-seven years of age, for God's sake *act* it . . .

Trofimov . . . What's my age got to do with it?

Mme Ranevsky . . . Because you're not a *man*, that's why.

Long pause. They stare at each other. TROFIMOV *is white with anger and perhaps a little fear.*

A man . . . should be capable of understanding . . . love. A man . . . needs it. Not to love *isn't* purity, it's weakness, it's fear, it's prudish, ridiculous and . . . abnormal . . .

Trofimov What are you saying?

Mme Ranevsky 'I am above love.' You're not *above* it, Peter, you're just not *up* to it. Why else would you be without a mistress, at twenty-seven?

Trofimov Are you really saying this? To me? (*Turns quickly towards the hall.*) Excuse me, will you . . .

Mme Ranevsky Peter . . .

Trofimov . . . No no, I'd prefer not to hear the rest, if you don't mind.

Mme Ranevsky Peter, wait . . .

TROFIMOV *leaves, returns almost at once.*

(*Pleading, a little desperate.*) Peter, I was joking... It was a *joke*, darling...

Trofimov What a pity then our relationship could not have ended on a better one.

He goes out into the hall. MME RANEVSKY *stands alone, facing in. We hear someone running quickly upstairs, then a crash as he falls.* ANYA *and* VARYA *shriek; then laughter.*

Mme Ranevsky What is it? What's happened?

ANYA *enters.*

Anya Petya's fallen down the stairs. (*Leaves laughing.*)

Mme Ranevsky So: he had the last laugh after all.

The STATIONMASTER *appears in the centre of the ballroom, framed by the arch, and begins to clear his throat. Dancers gather. Presently the orchestra will return to their places.* MME RANEVSKY *stands alone in the drawing-room facing him. For a moment it seems he's addressing her.*

Stationmaster A recitation entitled *The Sinner* by Alexei Tolstoy. The eponymous heroine is one Nadezdha Varkova, a young lady of good family whom fateful circumstance and impulsive desires conspire to turn into a fallen woman of doubtful virtue. *The Sinner.*

> She stands alone in darkened room
> And softly calls his name;
> But no one hears . . .

The orchestra strikes up a waltz. A dance begins. The STATIONMASTER *hovers for a moment, then retires with such dignity as he can muster.* ANYA *returns from the hall, drawing a slightly dishevelled* TROFIMOV *behind her.* VARYA *brings up the rear.*

Mme Ranevsky Dear dear boy, forgive me, please. Say you will. (*He bows stiffly, kisses her offered hand.*)

Come, we'll dance together . . .

They move off into the ballroom, followed by ANYA *and* VARYA, *who dance together.*

FIRS *hobbles into the drawing-room and props his stick against the door.* YASHA *enters from the billiard room to watch the dancing; notices* FIRS.

Yasha How are you, young whippersnapper?

Firs Not good. I've seen the day we had generals, admirals, barons dancing, now they send for post office clerks and stationmasters and even they have to be coaxed. I seem to have lost my strength somehow. The old master used to give us sealing wax for everything, whatever it was that ailed us. I've taken sealing wax every day for twenty years or more. I think it's that that's kept me going.

Yasha Grandad . . . you're a bore. (*Yawns*) You're ready for the knacker's yard.

Firs (*Deliberately*) Up yours, butterballs.

TROFIMOV *and* MME RANEVSKY *dance from ballroom to drawing-room.*

Mme Ranevsky Merci, mon beau. Let me rest a moment. I'm tired. (*She sits.*)

ANYA *in, excited.*

Anya A man in the kitchen says the orchard's been sold . . .

Mme Ranevsky To whom?

Anya He didn't say. He's gone now. (*To* TROFIMOV.) We should dance!

ANYA *and* TROFIMOV *whirl off into the ballroom.* MME RANEVSKY *sits very still.*

Yasha Kitchen gossip. Some old man passing the time of day.

Firs And Master Leon still not back. He's gone off in the thinnest of top-coats as though it were spring, if he's not careful he'll take a chill. Ach, these green young men!

Mme Ranevsky I can't breathe. Yasha, find out who bought it.

Yasha The old man left hours ago. (*He laughs suddenly.*)

Mme Ranevsky You think it funny? It pleases you, all this, does it?

Yasha It's that Epikhodov . . . he's such a clown. Million miseries, they call him.

Mme Ranevsky What about you, Firs. Where will you go, if the estate's sold?

Firs Where you order me, Ma'am.

Mme Ranevsky Are you unwell? You should go to bed if you're ill.

Firs (*Smiles ironically.*) Oh yes. And who'll serve you all and keep things going? There's only me for the whole house . . .

Yasha Madame Liuba, may I ask a favour of you. Should you return to Paris, may I have the honour of going with you? It's quite impossible I should be asked to stay here. (*Dropping voice.*) I'm sure you take my meaning – the lack of culture, the low level of moral refinement . . . the boredom . . . the food . . . and Firs here, stumbling around muttering his nonsense. I beg of you Ma'am: take me with you.

PISCHIK *in, enjoying himself, panting a little.*

Pischik Beautiful lady, permit me one tiny waltz, you're irresistible. (*He waltzes her round the room.*)

Now, sweetest Madam, could I interest you in a small loan? I find myself temporarily deficient of a trifling one hundred and eighty roubles . . .

He waltzes her off into the ballroom.

Yasha (*Ironic, to himself.*) Ah, what devotion!

In the ballroom CHARLOTTE *does cartwheels and forward and reverse handsprings, to cries of,* 'Bravo, Charlotte.' DUNYASHA, *red-faced and swooning with excitement, cascades down the steps into the drawing-room.* FIRS *clucks at her disapprovingly.*

Dunyasha It's the young mistress, she ordered me to. And there are men galore and hardly any of us and my brain's whirling and my heart's pounding and pounding. (*She sees her red face in the mirror; quickly begins to powder it.*)

That clerk, you know; the one from the post office, he whispered . . . things in my ear that almost made me swoon. It's true.

Firs Like what?

Dunyasha He said: You're like . . . a flower.

Yasha (*Leaving*) He's probably never seen one.

Dunyasha Like a flower . . . I have this delicate nature, you see, a delicate phrase can make me quiver with pleasure . . .

Firs Don't quiver too much, you'll break your stem.

Enter EPIKHODOV.

Epikhodov At least *look* at me . . . You turn away as though I were an earwig or something. This is no life!

Dunyasha You wanted something?

Epikhodov All right, you may not be wrong. Naturally, if you insist on looking at things from your own point of view – if you'll pardon my putting it this way and with such forcefulness – it becomes clear at once that it's you who've brought me to this . . . state. I know what my life is like, every day I befall some new misery. I've known it for so long I can even smile at it, once in a while. (*Pause*)

But you did give me your word, Dunyasha, in spite of . . .

Dunyasha . . . Do you think we could discuss it later? I'd rather you left me in peace just now. I'm in something of a dream just now, you see. (*She plays with her fan.*)

Epikhodov Every day sees a new horror engulf me and yet, forgive me for saying it, I simply smile at it all. (*Pause*) Sometimes I even laugh . . .

VARYA *in from the ballroom, a relentless broom.*

Varya (*To* EPIKHODOV.) Haven't you gone yet? There's not an ounce of respect in your whole body, is there. (*Seeing* DUNYASHA.) Out! (DUNYASHA *runs off.*)

First you wreck the billiard room, now you're lounging in the drawing-room like one of the guests.

Epikhodov You have no right to reprimand me, let me make that quite clear here and now . . .

Varya I am *not* reprimanding you, I'm merely telling you that you spend all your time wandering from one room to another and never lifting a finger, that's all. As a rule, clerks are expected to *work* – why else would one keep one?

Epikhodov Whether I work, walk, stand, sit or play billiards, those who sit in judgement of me will need to be considerably older and more sapient than you, M'mselle . . .

Varya How dare you speak to me that way. (*Wildly angry.*) You dare to suggest I don't know what I'm talking about? Get out! Go on, get out, now, at once, do you hear?

Epikhodov Please, I beg you, if you could just mollify your language a little . . .

Varya Out! Out! Get out this instant! (*He backs away towards the door. She follows him, beside herself.*)

You . . . million miseries! I don't want to see you in here again, is that understood!

EPIKHODOV *leaves. From behind the door we hear:* 'A complaint will be filed in due course on this matter.'

Are you going or aren't you? (*She grabs* FIRS's *stick from behind the door, raises it above her head.*)

All right, I'm ready for you. What's keeping you? In you come then . . .

LOPAKHIN *enters, a bottle of cognac sticking out from the pocket of his fur coat. She brings the stick down, he swerves to avoid it, it catches the side of his head and bounces off his shoulder. They stare at each other.*

Lopakhin (*Smiling, puzzled.*) Very kind of you.

Varya (*Breathless; far from recovered.*) I'm sorry.

Lopakhin No no. I've had worse welcomes in my time. On the whole, one of the better ones.

Varya Please. You'll be thanking me next. (*She goes to leave, placing stick by door; turns back into the room.*)

Did I hurt you?

Lopakhin Not at all.

He touches the side of his head, lurches a little, grips the back of a chair to steady himself. VARYA *lets out the tiniest of shrieks.* LOPAKHIN *straightens, grinning broadly at her, pleased with himself. She smiles back, tentative, uncertain, liking and fearing it.*

People swell into the ballroom. LOPAKHIN's *name buzzes around the house.*

PISCHIK *leads the pack.*

Pischik He's here! The man himself. (*He hugs* LOPAKHIN, *kisses him heavily on the lips.*)

Mmm. Just the slightest hint of cognac on the breath, my dear fellow. Never mind, we've been having fun here too . . .

Mme Ranevsky (*Appearing at last.*) What took you so long, Alex? Where's Leon?

Lopakhin Leon's here. Came back with me . . .

Mme Ranevsky (*Very still; breathless.*) Well then? The auction, what happened? Tell me everything.

Lopakhin (*Embarrassment masking elation.*) The auction finished at four. But we missed the train and had to wait till nine for the next one . . . Shaa . . . It's made me a little light in the head . . .

GAYEV comes in, weeping steadily, snuffling, carrying parcels.

Mme Ranevsky Leon. What happened? . . . For God's sake, will someone tell me and hurry up about it!

Gayev (*Waving a hand in her direction, handing parcel to* FIRS.) Here, take these . . . Now that's er . . . anchovies and . . . herrings in kirsch and er . . . I haven't eaten a thing all day . . . That's it . . . What I've endured today . . .

From the billiard room, distinctly, the click of balls and YASHA *calling a break:* 'Eighteen and seven make twenty-five.' GAYEV *grows calm as he listens.*

I'm tired. (*Pause. A deep vacancy has settled on him.*) Help me, Firs, will you . . .

GAYEV leaves through the ballroom, FIRS *in his wake.*

Pischik (*To* LOPAKHIN.) So tell us what happened at the auction, man.

LOPAKHIN says nothing, his hand on the neck of the bottle.

Mme Ranevsky Is it sold?

Lopakhin (*Turning to face her.*) Yes?

Mme Ranevsky To whom?

Lopakhin (*Simply*) Me.

MME RANEVSKY steadies herself against a table, stunned. VARYA *very quietly removes the keys from her belt, throws them into the middle of the room and leaves.*

LOPAKHIN wades through the others until he reaches the steps.

Lopakhin If you'd be so kind, ladies and gentlemen. Thank you. Thank you.

They part as though for a leper. He stands on the top step, looks down on the group. MME RANEVSKY *has sat down on the chair at the table, her face white and still.*

I'm sorry, you'll have to excuse me, my head's still whirling from it all . . .

He begins to laugh, nervous, elated.

All right then. We get to the auction, Deriganov's already in position.

Right off he tops Mr Gayev's fifteen thousand with a straight bid of thirty on top of the arrears. So there it was. I took him on. Forty thousand. He bid forty-five. Fifty-five. He bid sixty. I'm bidding in tens, he's hitting me with fives. Fine. We reach ninety thousand roubles and he's out! Withdraws! I have it! It's mine. The cherry orchard is mine!

He laughs out loud, takes the bottle from his pocket, sups deep.

All right, tell me I'm drunk, crazy, imagining every last bit of it . . .

He breaks into a strange stamping peasant dance, his bright boots flashing in the bright room.

. . . but don't laugh too soon, friends . . . Don't ever laugh at *me* again! (*Turns*) Musicians, where are you, let there be music then . . .

They're not to be seen. Their instruments lie about their chairs. The leader appears, stares at LOPAKHIN *a moment, then retires.*

Where are you, Father, Grandfather, get up from your graves and see me *now*, the one you kicked and starved and sent around half-naked in the snow . . . It's *me* . . . the man himself . . . and I've just bought this estate and you won't find a finer one anywhere in the world! I've bought the estate you were both serfs on, where you weren't even allowed inside the kitchen. Do you hear me? Eh? Ha! You think I'm imagining it, dreaming it . . . oh these ignorant yearnings . . . is that it? (*He strides down into the drawing-room, collects the keys from the floor.*)

She threw away the keys, to show her reign is ended . . . (*The orchestra returns, begins tuning up.*)

. . . Hey, musicians, let's have some music, I want to hear you . . . a legzinka for the people . . . who have come to see how the dull and lowly Lopakhin will take his axe to the cherry orchard and send the trees whistling to the ground! And . . . summer cottages we'll build in their stead and our children's children's children will hear the distant music of a new life blossoming about them . . . Music! There must be music!

The orchestra begins the spry legzinka. The room empties around LOPAKHIN, *who seems wholly unaware of it.* PISCHIK *remains; and* MME RANEVSKY, *whose head rests on her steepled hands. She makes no sound, no movement.* LOPAKHIN *sees her finally, focuses frowningly. Approaches her, at a loss now for the words.*

Lopakhin Why? Why? Why? (*Pause*) Why didn't you hear me? (*Pause*) There's no way back, friend. (*Pause. Moved by her stillness.*) Why do I have to be the cause of your pain? Why can't we somehow . . . rebuild these awkward, crumbling lives . . . ?

Pischik (*Softly, his arm in* LOPAKHIN'*s.*) Ssh now. Let's leave her to her sadness . . . Come. (*Leads him gently to the ballroom.*)

LOPAKHIN *snaps from his daze in the centre of the ballroom. Notices that the music has tailed away.*

Lopakhin What's this then? I said music. Play. If I *want* music, let there *be* music. (*They strike up again. Ironic.*)

This is the new master speaking, the owner of the cherry orchard. (*He lumbers against a small table, knocks a lit candelabra to the floor.* PISCHIK *stamps it carefully out.*) Leave it! I can pay!

He leaves with PISCHIK.

MME RANEVSKY *sits alone in the drawing-room. The musicians play some moments longer, watching the doorway rather nervously, stop finally, case their instruments and leave.* MME RANEVSKY *begins to weep now, very softly, undistractedly.* ANYA *and* TROFIMOV *enter quickly.* ANYA *kneels at her mother's feet.* TROFIMOV *stays inside the archway.*

Anya Mother Mother Mother don't good gentle precious Mother I love you let me bless you here here don't don't cry please it's gone now it's sold all right but you're alive good and pure and whole with a life to live come come with me come we'll go away from here grow new things better finer than these and then you'll see how right all this has been and fulfilment will smile on your skin like evening sunlight and you'll breathe again Mother I promise I promise.

MME RANEVSKY *has stopped weeping. Stares now into* ANYA's *eyes.* TROFIMOV *shakes his head slowly, leaves.*

Tape: (ANYA's *voice*): '«Пойдём, милая! Пойдём!..»

BLACK.

ACT IV

Black.

Tape: (YASHA's *voice*): «Простóй нарóд порщáться пришёл.»

Lights up, harsh and bright on the bare white nursery. Nothing of furniture or decoration remains save for a huddle of pieces in a corner marked 'sale'. Trunks, bags and bundles mound about the door and the back wall.

LOPAKHIN *stands in the middle of the room, staring at the door, which is open.*

YASHA *stands by the window, a tray of champagne and glasses in his hands. The glasses are full and flattening.*

Odd voices – VARYAS's, ANYA's *– flit through the house.*

EPIKHODOV *drags a trunk in through the door, a piece of looped rope to tie it with in his hand. He places the loop round his neck to stand on the recalcitrant trunk to close it.* VARYA *in briefly, ignores* LOPAKHIN's *wave at the tray, reads the room, stares pointedly at* EPIKHODOV, *leaves.* EPIKHODOV *frowns, half-attempts a mute explanation, gets down, goes out after her.*
A cheer from outside. GAYEV's *voice grows out of it:* 'Thank you, dear people, thank you.'

Yasha It's the rural idiots come to say good-bye. If you want my opinion, it is that the common folk have big hearts but tiny brains.

Silence. LOPAKHIN *stares on at the door, ignoring him.* MME RANEVSKY *enters,* GAYEV *following.* MME RANEVSKY *is pale, on edge.*

Gayev . . . but not the whole purse, Liuba. You can't go on like that, it's too much . . .

Mme Ranevsky . . . I couldn't help it, all right. (*Deliberately*) It couldn't be helped . . .

She skirts him quickly, leaves. He follows her. LOPAKHIN *has indicated the champagne but been ignored.*

Lopakhin (*Following to doorway.*) A glass of champagne? Won't you join me in one farewell glass? Dear friends, I beg of you . . . I didn't think to bring any from town and I could find only one bottle at the station . . . Still, we could have a glass together . . . (*Returning from door.*) It seems I didn't need to buy any . . . Fine. I'll abstain with you.

YASHA *places the tray down carefully on a chair.*

Have a glass yourself, Yasha.

Yasha (*Toasting*) To those who journey, to those who wave them off. (*Drains glass.*) Not the real thing, I'm afraid. Pity, that.

Lopakhin Eight roubles a bottle anyway. It's bloody cold in here today.

Yasha No one bothered with stoves today. Not that it matters. Since we're going. (*He laughs.*)

Lopakhin Something funny?

Yasha Just happy.

Lopakhin Look at it, October, and smooth as summer out there. Building weather. (*Checks watch, calls through open door.*) The train leaves in forty-six minutes precisely, ladies and gentlemen. (*Silence*)

So we should leave in . . . twenty minutes, I think. (*Silence*)

Please . . . hurry.

TROFIMOV *enters, in an old battered overcoat, from outside.*

Trofimov You know, I think it's time we were off . . . the carriage has arrived. God knows where my overshoes have got to – thin air. (*Calling through door.*) Anya, have you seen my overshoes? I can't find them anywhere.

Lopakhin And I'm for Kharkov. I'll take the same train. I'll spend the winter there. I've spent too long sitting around here chattering, I need to be doing. I'm useless, if I'm not working; don't know what to do with my hands – (*flaps them, serious and comic*) – look at them – they just hang, like someone else's . . .

Trofimov Well, we'll be gone soon and you'll be able to get back to your valuable labours again . . .

Lopakhin (*Indicating glasses.*) Fancy a small one? (TROFIMOV *shakes his head.*)

So, you're off to Moscow then.

Trofimov Ahunh. I'll go as far as town with them. And tomorrow I go to Moscow.

Lopakhin Mmm. No doubt the university's delaying the start of the session till you get there?

Trofimov I can't see why it should concern you.

Lopakhin How many years is it now you've been a student . . . ?

Trofimov That the best you can do? You've worn it smooth, man. (*Resumes the hunt for his overshoes.*) By the way, it's unlikely we'll meet again; so let me give you a piece of advice by way of farewell: try not waving your arms about – it's a bad habit, arm-waving. And this talk about building summer cottages, all these visionary predictions that their tenants will one day become their owners, that's all a kind of . . . arm-waving too.

Pause.

I say all this because . . . when all's said that can be . . . I like you. (*Pause*)

You have the hands of a painter, slender and full of grace; and a gentle, generous soul . . .

Lopakhin (*Embracing him warmly.*) Good-bye, then, little dove. And thank you. (*Looks at him, close up.*) What about money, let me give you some for the journey.

Trofimov What for? I've no need of it.

Lopakhin You haven't a penny.

Trofimov Yes I have. I just got some for a translation. (*Pats his pocket.*) It's here. (*Looks around the room.*) Overshoes are a different matter entirely . . .

A pair of rubber overshoes fly across the room, flung from the doorway. VARYA's *voice follows them.* 'Take the filthy things!'

Trofimov Ah, such shy and gentle charms. Mmm. (*Picks up overshoes.*) These aren't mine!

Lopakhin I put out a thousand acres of poppy last spring and I got in a clear forty thousand profit . . . that's something to behold, I can tell you, a poppy field in bloom . . . Anyway, the point is I made the forty thousand and you're welcome to a loan because I'm flush, you see . . . (*Pause*) And there's no point being 'proud' about it. You're dealing with a peasant, son of a peasant . . . just that . . .

Trofimov . . . And you're dealing with the son of a chemist's assistant. Which means nothing either. (LOPAKHIN *goes for his wallet.*)

Leave it, let it be . . . You could offer me two hundred thousand and I still wouldn't want it. I'm free of all that. All the things you all cherish and crave after – rich and poor alike – are for me no more than . . . flocculence . . . shimmering on the air. And because I have the will and . . . the pride . . . (*he smiles*) . . . I can go on without you, transcend you, if you like. Men are on the move, headed for the higher truths, the greater happiness, and I count myself an outrider for the expedition.

Lopakhin Will you get there?

Trofimov Oh yes. (*Pause*) Get there or show others the route.

An axe hits a tree, in the distance.

Lopakhin (*Hand out.*) Take care, little dove. (*Handclasp.*) Time for us to go.

Pause.

Seems to me we're both pretty good at striking poses . . . but life couldn't give a damn and carries on course regardless. When I've worked myself into the ground for days on end without rest, the pleasure it gives me half-persuades me I know why I'm alive. But Russia is overflowing with people who see no purpose at all to their existence. (*Pause*) But . . . maybe that's not the point either. (*Pause*) They say Mr Gayev has taken the position in the bank – six thousand a year, they say. Won't hang on to it, shouldn't wonder; too . . . idle . . .

Anya (*From doorway.*) Mother says will you not let them cut down the orchard until we've gone.

Trofimov (*Leaving through hall.*) Tact, Lopakhin. Where's your tact?

Lopakhin Of course, of course. My god, these workmen . . .

Follows TROFIMOV

Anya Have they taken Firs to hospital?

Yasha I left instructions for this morning. I'm sure he's gone.

Anya (*To* EPIKHODOV, *in doorway.*) Simon Epikhodov. Please make sure Firs has been taken to the hospital . . .

Yasha Yegov was told to do it this morning. Why go on about it?

Epikhodov In my definitive opinion, the ancient Firs is beyond medicine and should make ready to join his ancestors. For my part . . . I can but envy him.

He's placed a suitcase on a hatbox, squashing it flat. Stares at it, nodding several times. Turns to see DUNYASHA *in doorway, looking at* YASHA, *who's turned his back on her. Stares up at the heavens, gestures at the crushed hatbox, smiles resignedly at his 'fate', walks dolefully off.*

Yasha . . . Nine hundred and ninety-nine thousand nine hundred and ninety-nine . . .

Varya (*From the hall.*) Has Firs been taken to the hospital?

Anya Yes.

Varya Then why is the letter for the doctor still here?

Anya I don't know. I'll send someone after them with it . . .

She leaves.

DUNYASHA *has busied herself rather fussily with items of baggage. She now approaches* YASHA.

Dunyasha Yasha. Please look at me. You're going, aren't you . . . you're deserting me, aren't you . . .

She tries to put her arms around his neck, but he detaches them with practised ease, a glass of champagne in his hand.

Yasha No need for tears, girl. In under a week I'll be back home in Paris. Tomorrow we'll join the Pullman and Zzam, we'll shoot across Europe like a bullet. Isn't it incredible. (*He dedahs the Marseillaise.*) This is no place for me, there's no life here, nothing happens here. I'm full up to here of . . . backwardness and mediocrity. Up to here. (*Another glass disappears.*) For God's sake don't cry, girl. Behave yourself and you'll have no need of tears.

Dunyasha Write to me, won't you. From Paris. (*Begins to powder her face.*) You know how I've loved you, Yasha. I've been good to you, Yasha. You know how . . . soft I am . . .

Yasha Shh, someone's coming.

He unlocks a suitcase swiftly, repositions it, begins to lock it again.

MME RANEVSKY *comes in, with* GAYEV *and* CHARLOTTE.

Gayev We really ought to be going, Liuba, it's getting late . . . (*Stares at* YASHA.) Who's smelling of herring in here? . . .

Mme Ranevsky . . . Ten minutes and then we shall leave. (*Surveys the room swiftly.*) Good-bye, house. Old Grandfather. Winter, spring . . . and you'll be gone too, they'll have pulled you down. (*Reflective, rather cool.*) And you've seen it all, old walls, haven't you? (*Kisses* ANYA, *embraces her.*) Ah, *mon petit trésor*, how brilliantly you glow, you have . . . diamonds in your eyes. You're happy, aren't you? Are you?

Anya Yes, Mama. It's like being born again.

Gayev Absolutely. Everything's as it should be now. How depressed we all were before the orchard went . . . what we all endured. But now it's all done with . . . irreversible . . . everyone's calm and cheerful once again. I hold an office in a bank now, a financier you might say . . . Red into the middle . . . tla . . . and you look so much better too, Liuba, all in all. No doubt about it.

Mme Ranevsky (*Being helped into her coat and hat.*) Yes, I'm calmer, it's true. And sleeping again at night. Yasha, my things, it's time.

YASHA *begins carrying her cases, etc., outside.*

(*To* ANYA.) We'll be together again very soon, my baby. I'll live in Paris for a little while on the money your great-aunt sent us to buy the estate – God bless Yaroslavl – but that won't last forever . . .

Anya Come back soon. You will, won't you . . . I'll work hard and pass all my exams and then I'll be ready to work for you. We'll devour whole libraries together, you and me, won't we . . . (*kissing her hand*) . . . on autumn evenings; we'll learn new things for this . . . new life . . .

Mme Ranevsky I'll be back, golden one.

CHARLOTTE *begins crooning.* LOPAKHIN *enters.*

Gayev Charlotte's happy, too. She's singing.

CHARLOTTE *picks up a bundle* (TROFIMOV'S *overshoes wrapped in a cloth*), *holds it like a swaddled baby.*

Charlotte Bye bye my baby.

The bundle cries twice.

. . . Shh sweet little boy, there there . . . (*Further cries.*)

. . . Yes, it's not fair is it, my darling. (*She drops the bundle without looking at it.*)

I shall need a new post. I can't survive without one.

Lopakhin I'll find you something, Charlotte. No need to worry yourself.

Gayev So, everyone's abandoning us . . . Varya . . . suddenly no one wants us any more.

Charlotte There's nowhere for me in town. I shall have to leave the area. (*Hums*) Ach, I don't really care.

PISCHIK *enters, red, sweating, breathless.*

Lopakhin My god, it's the eighth wonder of the world!

Pischik Oooph . . . let me get my breath back . . . I'm done for . . . Dear friends, water, please . . .

Gayev Water first, then a loan, I suppose. Forgive me, I have to go . . . (*Leaves*)

Pischik (*Mopping face and neck, seated on a box.*) Ah, dear lady, so long since I saw you . . . (*Sees* LOPAKHIN.) And you . . . glad to see you . . . a man of the highest discernment . . . Here, this is for you – (*hands money to* LOPAKHIN) – four hundred roubles. That leaves eight hundred and forty still outstanding . . .

DUNYASHA *brings a glass of water, which he swigs straight off. She pours him another.*

Lopakhin (*Stares at the money.*) Am I dreaming this? Where did it come from?

Pischik Please, a moment. (*Swigging*) That's better. Something quite extraordinary happened. Some English folk called at my place and discovered some sort of white . . . clay on my land . . . (*To* MME RANEVSKY.) And four hundred for you, my . . . marvellous . . . madam . . . (*hands her money*) . . . the rest later. (*Another glass of water, splashing drops down his neck.*) This fellow I was talking to just now on the train says that some great philosopher or other seriously urges people to jump off roofs. 'Jump off roofs,' he says, 'and your worries are over.' What about that then? More water, please . . .

Lopakhin These English . . .

Pischik Oh yes. I gave a twenty-four year lease on the land where the clay is. (*Standing, a bunch of currency notes in his fist.*) And now you'll kindly excuse me, I must trot along, got to see Znoikov . . . and Kardamonov . . . pay my debts, you know. (*Drains glass.*) Good health to all here . . . . Probably drop round Thursday . . .

Mme Ranevsky We're just about to move into town and tomorrow I'll be en route for France.

Pischik Town?

Long silence. He scans the room, the baggage, the coats.

Oh yes. The furniture and erm. (*Long pause.*) Luggage. Yes, I see. No matter. (*He weeps very quietly, with no attempt to hide or dissemble it.*)

Can't be helped. These . . . English, men of the highest discernment, you know. Never mind. Everything you wish yourselves, and God go with you. Nothing lives without it dies. (*Kisses* MME RANEVSKY'*s hand.*) So, when you hear they've put *me* under, remember the old horse and say, 'I used to know the creature – Pischik, he was called – God be with him!' Isn't this splendid weather? Yes . . .

He goes out, returns at once.

Dashenka sends regards. (*Leaves*)

Mme Ranevsky Now we can go. Two things bother me. Firs is sick . . . (*Checks watch.*) Perhaps a couple of minutes longer . . .

Anya Mother, Firs has been driven to the hospital. Yasha saw to it this morning.

Mme Ranevsky . . . And Varya. Rising early and working late is her life; without it she'll be like a fish in sand. She's grown so thin and wan and . . . tearful. Poor Varya. (*Pause*) You do know, Alex, that I'd always dreamt of giving her to you . . . And all the signs were that you would take her.

She gestures something to ANYA, *who takes* CHARLOTTE *by the sleeve and leads her out of the room.*

She loves you, you know . . . and I know you're not . . . unfond of her . . . I can't see at all why you both keep . . . so separate. It doesn't make sense.

LOPAKHIN *stares at her for a long time, carefully suppressing, but at cost. what he most wants to say. Finally:*

Lopakhin No, I'm sure you're right. It *is* . . . very confusing. (*Pause*) If there's still the time, why not, we could settle it now and get it over with. Once *you*'ve . . . gone, I'll never do it.

Mme Ranevsky Wonderful idea, it won't take a minute, let me call her . . .

Lopakhin There's even champagne, to mark the occasion. (*Glances at glasses.*) Or there was. (YASHA *coughs discreetly.*) *You* could drink it by the bucket, couldn't you?

Mme Ranevsky (*Excited now.*) It doesn't matter. We'll leave you alone. Yasha, *allez*!

YASHA *leaves quickly on the sharp command.*

(*Calling*) Varya, come here, will you . . .

VARYA *calls something.*

. . . No, leave that and come in here. Quickly girl.

She goes out into the hall. LOPAKHIN *looks at his watch, then carefully turns each glass upside down in turn, to check their dryness. Some whispering in the hall.* VARYA *arrives finally, begins at once to check the luggage against a list in her hand. Silence. Then:*

Varya That's odd, I just can't seem to (see it . . .).

Lopakhin What's that?

Varya . . . I packed it this morning, where is it? . . .

Silence.

Lopakhin Where do you go now, Varya?

Varya What? Oh, to the Rogulins. I said I'd go and look after things there. A sort of housekeeper, I suppose.

Lopakhin That's er . . . that's Yashnyevo, isn't it?

Varya Mmmm.

Lopakhin What's that, fifty miles? (*Long pause.*) So. It's all over, here . . .

Varya (*Searching again.*) . . . It's here somewhere . . . Unless I put it with the trunk . . . (*To* LOPAKHIN.) Yes, that's right. There's nothing else now . . .

Lopakhin And I'm away to Kharkov directly . . . I catch the next train. (*Rubs his finger on a glass edge.*) There's plenty to do there. I'll leave Epikhodov here . . . I've taken him on, you know.

Varya (*Disdain beneath the cool neutral tone.*) Have you.

Lopakhin This time last year we'd had snow . . . Remember? Just look at that sun. (*Pause*) Still, it's cold enough. Frost on the grass there . . .

Varya Is there? I haven't looked. (*Pause*) Our thermometer's broken, as it happens . . .

Silence. They stare at each other briefly, then look away. Someone calls, 'Mr Lopakhin, Mr Lopakhin,' from outside the house.

Lopakhin (*Nods slowly, calls.*) Yes. I'm here.

He leaves, quite quickly, but with no sense of scurry. VARYA *sits down very slowly on a bundle in the corner of the room. Stares out into space, seeing nothing, her hands on her breasts, the fingers almost touching the wooden cross between them.*

MME RANEVSKY *enters quietly, searches for her, sees her.*

Mme Ranevsky Well? (*Pause.* VARYA *doesn't move.*) We have to go.

Varya (*Getting up.*) Yes, I know. (*Straightening her belt and hair.*) I should make the Rogulins this evening, If I don't miss the train . . .

Mme Ranevsky (*Calling through the doorway.*) Anya, put your things on.

ANYA *in, with* GAYEV *and* CHARLOTTE, *ready for off.* GAYEV *wears a thick topcoat with a hood.* SERVANTS *and* COACHMEN *crowd the room.* EPIKHODOV *sputters around the luggage.*

Mme Ranevsky Good. (*Drily*) Let the journey commence!

Anya Ready, ready . . .

Gayev My friends, dear, loving friends. Now, on the brink of departing this house forever, no one will insist that I keep silent . . . For how can I not express to you all, as I bid you farewell, the emotions that swell up in my heart (and swamp me with their) . . .

Anya Uncle!

Varya (*Quiet*) No, Uncle. Please.

Gayev (*At once.*) Double the red into the middle. (*Finger to lip.*) See, shh, nothing.

Enter TROFIMOV, *then* LOPAKHIN.

Trofimov All aboard, ladies and gentlemen, time to go.
Lopakhin Epikhodov – coat!

Movement begins. It lacks order, eddies and dribbles, here and there.

Mme Ranevsky Give me one minute. One minute.

She stands in the centre of the room. Takes it in.

I feel as if I'm seeing this room, this house, for the first time. Those walls, this ceiling . . . all new . . . I'm suddenly filled with a terrible . . . greed for them . . .
Gayev (*Very clearly.*) I remember when I was six years old I sat at that window one Feast Day and watched my father striding off to church . . .
Mme Ranevsky (*Surveying floor, now cleared of luggage.*) Is that it then?
Lopakhin Yes. I think so. (*To* EPIKHODOV.) You're in charge while I'm gone, all right?
Epikhodov (*Croaking*) It's in good hands, never fear.
Lopakhin What're you whispering for?
Epikhodov I drank some water a moment ago. I must've swallowed something.
Yasha What a clown!
Mme Ranevsky You'll leave it empty, then?
Lopakhin Till the spring.

VARYA *pulls an umbrella from a bundle of clothes, appears menacing for a moment.* LOPAKHIN *feigns a tactical retreat.*

Varya (*Very quiet, contained.*) There's no need for that . . . You won't get hurt.
Trofimov Let's go then. Into the carriage *now* or we miss the train.
Varya (*Seeing his overshoes in* CHARLOTTE's *doll.*) Peter, your overshoes . . . (*She picks them up, hands them to him.*) Look at them, they're falling apart . . .
Trofimov (*Putting them on.*) Last call for the carriage!
Gayev (*Suddenly distressed and disorientated.*) The train, the station . . . spot into the middle, double the white into the bottom, click, chuck . . .
Mme Ranevsky We're going
Lopakhin All out? No one left behind? (*Locks a door.*) I've stored some things in there, best to keep it locked. Right!
Anya (*Cheerful*) 'Bye, old house. 'Bye old life.
Trofimov And a big . . . hell . . . o . . . o – (*he throws the echo round the house*) – to tomorrow.

They leave together. VARYA *glances at the room and leaves.* YASHA *and* CHARLOTTE *and her dog follow.*

Lopakhin (*To* GAYEV.) Till spring then. (*To* MME RANEVSKY.) Au . . . revoir?
. . . Is that how you say it?

He leaves.

GAYEV *and* MME RANEVSKY *stand in the room alone.* GAYEV *walks to her
side, puts his hand in hers, as a child might. They stand very still, side by
side, looking out. Sounds of hooves on gravel, snuffles, wheels rocking,
from outside, some calling.*

Anya (*Voice off, calling, happy.*) Mother!
Trofimov (*Voice off, some echo.*) Hello . . . o . . . o . . .
Gayev Sister . . .
Anya (*Voice off, calling*) Mother!
Trofimov (*Voice off, echoing it.*) Tomorrow . . . ow . . . ow . . . ow . . .

MME RANEVSKY *blinks, stirs, drop's* GAYEV'*s hand.*

Mme Ranevsky (*Calling*) Yes.

They leave.

*The room is empty, save for a solitary chair on the back wall. Sound of
doors being locked, carriages leaving.*

Silence.

An axe hits a tree, once, twice, three times.

Slow, shuffling footsteps. FIRS *enters, in jacket, white waistcoat, as ever,
but with slippers. He's ill. He crosses to the door, tries the handle.*

Firs Locked. They've gone.

There's a solitary chair left, its back broken. FIRS *painfully drags it into the
middle of the room, sits on it.*

They forgot me. Never mind. I'll sit here for a while.

He picks up the cloth that covered TROFIMOV'*s overshoes, shivering a
little, places it over his head and ears. The axe starts up again, closer.*

I don't imagine for one minute he's put his fur coat on . . . No, no . . .
he'll be wearing the thin one . . . (*He blows on his hands.*) . . . If I don't
see to it . . . mmm? These green lads . . .

Mutters, unintelligibly, for a moment. The axe persists, closing in.

. . . It's gone . . . it's gone . . . as if I'd never lived it . . . (*Looks at the
floor.*) I might lie down in a minute. You've no strength left in you, have
you . . . you've nothing left, eh . . . you've nothing . . .

*He begins to rock backwards and forwards in the chair, slowly at first, but
the arcs grow longer, the legs lifting front and back.*

You silly old nothing. Silly old nothing. Silly old nothing.

The axe pounds towards the house. FIRS *rocks on, muttering.*
Tape: (FIRS's *voice*): «Недотёпа!» (*Over and over.*)

Cut, abruptly.

He topples to the floor, felled. The axe stops. A distant sound is heard. It's the sound of a snapping string.

BLACK